הַגָּדָה שֶׁל פֶּסַח

Leader's Guide for

A DIFFERENT NIGHT

By Noam Zion and David Dishon

מכון
שלום
הרטמן
**SHALOM
HARTMAN
INSTITUTE**

Library of Congress Catalog 96-71600
© Noam Zion and David Dishon
Published in the U.S.A. 1997

for U.S. orders: Haggadahs-R-Us
1888 S. Compton, Cleveland Hts., OH 44118
877-308-4175 • 216-321-6734 • fax 216-321-6717
thumpers@apk.net • www.haggadahsrus.com
author's e-mail: ZIONSACS@Netvision.net.il

"The real question is not why do we keep Passover but how do we continue to keep Passover year after year and keep it from becoming stultified!
How can we be privileged to plan it so that, as Rabbi Abraham Isaac Kook said, 'The old may become new and the new may become holy.'"

IRA STEINGROOT

"One must make changes on this night, so the children will notice and ask: 'Why is this night different?'"

MAIMONIDES

"Only the lesson which is enjoyed can be learned well."

JUDAH HANASI

Table of Contents

III. BACKGROUND ESSAYS

1 PART I

INSTRUCTIONS *for the* LEADER

 *Chapter 1*

A Guide for the Perplexed: Clarifying the Roles of the Leader of the Seder

■ *by Noam Zion*

The leaders of the seder often face contradictory demands from the heterogeneous "audience" at the table, on one hand, and from the Jewish tradition embodied in the Haggadah, on the other hand. Personally I feel like the conductor of a symphony orchestra with a complex operatic score to perform. The Haggadah jumps from one movement to the next with very disjointed transitions. The audience is made up of a diverse group: some dislike classical Jewish "music" altogether and many cannot read the Hebrew libretto. Others remember the masterly performance of a beloved grandparent, against which they measure my poor imitation and condemn my every innovation as an unforgiveable deviation. Non-Jewish guests and young children are totally unacquainted with the "program." The age range produces differing attention spans and many unscheduled intermissions. As for the hungry, and not-so-silent majority of the audience, they sometimes prefer to end the "concert" after the first overture rather than demanding encores. The guests at the seder are, in fact, meant to be the musicians, yet they are often reluctant to participate in the concert. They often struggle among themselves to shorten the score in the middle of the performance.

Yet everyone seems to have such high expectations of the seder. It is no surprise that I feel inadequate to the task at hand. After all, I am no rabbi. Yet my grandparents and all of Jewish tradition peer over my shoulder insisting I carry on the torch, doing it all as it has been done for generations and engaging the next generation to boot.

What is the leader's role at the seder? By what criteria must you judge the evening successful? How do you concentrate on the main goal and avoid getting distracted by the details? Rabbinic tradition offers three models for the seder leader:

(1) the **priest/rabbi** who is the *Master of Ceremonies*

(2) the **host of a symposium** who is a *Talk-Show Moderator*

(3) the **parent educator** who is a *Skilled Storyteller*

(1) The Priestly Seder:
Maintaining the Traditional Protocol

The final poem of the seder (חֲסַל סִדּוּר פֶּסַח כְּהִלְכָתוֹ) declares: *"We have concluded the seder performed according to all the standards of Jewish law."* It reflects the satisfaction of priestly/rabbinic leaders who have completed all the steps of the seder on time without skipping anything. They fulfilled their duties not only to religious law but to the age-old tradition of their grandparents. It was "done right," with the same conscientiousness with which the priests once conducted the Pesach sacrifice in the Temple. Even though the age of sacrifices is over, the Rabbis codified the "seder" — which means "the order of rites" — to allow lay persons to transform their homes into miniature Temples. After a religiously meticulous purification of the house from chametz, the leaders become the stand-in for the priest at this home service. Since Pesach is the covenant renewal ceremony of the Jewish people, the punishment for a Seder improperly performed is figuratively *karet* — to be cut off from one's people.

In the twentieth century, rabbis are often hired to serve priestly roles in synagogue rites, but on Pesach the home is the synagogue and each parent must become the **master of Jewish ceremonies**. Even if we are lax on kashrut or holiday observance generally, Pesach is not to be taken lightly. It cannot be just a social get-together. The table must become a kind of altar, and the atmosphere must be more formal, more sanctified. However, choosing the priestly/rabbinic role often means fighting a rear guard action against all those who want to "get to the food already." Many leaders think that the seder requires them to read all the Hebrew even if incomprehensible. Under time pressure, the priest-in-us may squelch adult discussions and postpone the need to dramatize the story for the children. In the name of the demands of tradition, innovations may seem threatening. The priestly leader may feel that without faithfully sticking to the order, the family seder will disintegrate and with it perhaps the family cohesiveness.

In appreciation of that impulse, *A Different Night* contains the complete traditional Haggadah with expanded directions for performing halachically mandated rituals, but it also contains much more. It offers adults and children both the stimulation of good discussion and the pleasure of a good story.

(2) The Symposium:
A Lively, Thoughtful Discussion

The Rabbis envisioned an additional role for the leader of the seder very different from the religious legalist. They sought a gracious and sophisticated host of a symposium. The meal, for Greek upper classes and for Rabbinic scholars alike, was a place for intellectual discussion — serious and light at once.

While reclining on couches (living room in Greek is *tri-clinium* — three beds or couches), sipping wine (*"symposium"* means "drinking together"), and dipping vegetables in appetizing sauces, the host would propose a topic for discussion such as the nature of love (as in Plato's *Symposium*) or the origins of the holiday being celebrated. Later the celebrants would sing songs to praise the Divine. The qualities demanded of the leader remind us of a top-notch talk-show moderator:

> The leader of the symposium "took pride in gathering about him many persons of culture and entertaining them with conversation ... now proposing topics worthy of enquiry, now disclosing solutions of his own; for he never put his questions without previous study or in a haphazard way, but with the utmost critical, even Socratic acumen, so that all admired the keen observation showed by his question."
>
> (ATHENAEUS, DEIPNOSOPHISTS, 2ND C. GREECE)

> "Questions should be easy, the problems plain and familiar, not intricate and dark, so that they may neither vex the unlearned nor frighten them from speaking up ... the discourse should be like our wine, common to all, of which everyone may equally partake."

> "A symposium is a communion of serious and mirthful entertainment, discourse and symbolic actions .... (It furthers) a deeper insight into the points debated at the table. For the memory of the pleasures arising from the food is shortlived ... but the subjects of philosophical queries and discussions remain always fresh after they have been imparted."
>
> (PLUTARCH, QUAESTIONES, 2ND C. GREECE AND ROME)

The Rabbis, like the Greeks, loved to delve into the classics (Torah and Homer respectively) and derive philosophic insights. In the Haggadah the Biblical text *"Arami Oved Avi"* ("A Wandering Aramean," Deuteronomy 26) is the opening gambit and around it the Rabbis weaved "oral explications." This free-wheeling oral commentary is called **agadah** — one of the origins of the word **haggadah**. In Rabbinic symposia, playful and insightful comments were called for, as well as attempts to connect the classical texts to contemporary political events. (Some scholars say that the five rabbis who spent all night discussing the Exodus texts in Bnai B'rak were also laying the foundations for the Bar Kochba Revolt against the Roman Empire, 132 C.E.)

What would it mean to lead a seder as a rabbinic/philosophic symposium? First, the leaders would have to loosen up their exclusive focus on *reading* the Haggadah out loud. After all, *"haggadah"* does **not** mean book, it means oral commentary and discussion. The sample of Rabbinic commentary — *Arami Oved Ami* — found in the Haggadah would be viewed as just one of many possible ways to deal with the question of the evening: what is freedom?

Second, the measure of success would be the ability to engage as many participants as possible in the intellectual debate. Guests might be asked to prepare a short provocative contribution of their own. Questions, well-posed, would dominate rather than mere recitations of the text. The leaders would be judged not by their religious knowledge, but their ability to facilitate a general conversation about the Exodus and its contemporary significance.

No doubt this role definition is challenging. But that is precisely what the Rabbis wanted. They codified the ideal that every family hold a miniature Rabbinic symposium on Pesach, just as they codified the requirements to eat a precise minimum of maror and drink four cups of wine. Clearly the spirit of this Haggadah — *A Different Night* — encourages innovative discussions of this sort for all types of families, whatever their background. These "innovations" are in fact a return to the authentic Rabbinic seder.

The symposium model also has its drawbacks, however. It will be a longer seder, though more interesting and more participatory. Significant hors d'oeuvres must precede and accompany the discussion to prevent growling stomachs from drowning out the conversation. This model may be mistakenly perceived as a deviation from time honored Jewish traditions, so the leader must explain to the guests what will be different and why. Be aware that the focus on issues of interest to adults and perhaps older adolescents may go right over the heads of the children. Therefore it is important to balance between the symposium model and the storytelling model of the seder.

(3) The Storytellers' Seder

The seder leaders are also **parent educators**. The biblical origin of the word *"haggadah"* echoes the commandment: *"v'higad'ta"* — "you shall tell your child." (EXODUS 13:8) True, since the days of the Rabbis formal Jewish education has been transferred from the parent to the teacher. Nevertheless, on Pesach night the parents are expected to reclaim their birth-right as primary Jewish educators for they have a family story of rescue to retell. **Not knowledge, primarily, but empathy is required**. The task is to dramatize the story so that "in every generation you shall see yourself as if you went out of Egypt." Only personal witnessing can transmit identification. In this spirit *A Different Night* suggests the leader ask the participants to retell personal stories of danger and escape, of enslavement and liberation, alongside the Exodus tale.

The parent educators must take their clues from the Haggadah but go beyond its recitation. For example, the singing of the four questions is not really enough. The Rabbis require parents to elicit real questions. Evoking them requires departing from the "seder" — the set ritual order — in order to create surprise and curiosity. That is the origin of the name *A Different Night* for as Maimonides explains: *One must make changes on this night, so the children will notice and ask: "Why is this night different?"*

The story of Exodus is mentioned over and over in the traditional Haggadah but never told. The Rabbis assumed the parent would **tell** — not read — the story at the appropriate level for each child. Therefore *A Different Night* adds children's versions of the Exodus as well as adult ones in order to facilitate the most central commandment of the evening. Ironically, those priestly leaders of the seder who mistakenly read only what the traditional Haggadah includes have not "completed the seder rite according to all its laws." They have forgotten to field the children's real questions and to retell the story dramatically.

Conclusion

So much is expected of the leaders of the seder. Yet the majority of them are neither knowledgeable priests/rabbis, nor educated philosophers at home in a symposium, nor professionally trained teachers with pedagogic skills for handling the mercilessly heterogeneous "audience" at the seder. **The haggadah is meant to be a manual for home education.** It must provide the ritual order and directions for the lay priest as well as provocative questions, choice remarks and cute anecdotes for the talk-show host at the home symposium. In addition, it should offer gimmicks to arouse curiosity and well-told tales for the untrained parent educator. This has been the task of the authors of **A Different Night** — to provide a varied resource book to match the diverse roles of the leader of the seder.

What the leader of the seder must decide is how to use these resources. Is this year's list of guests and relatives most in need of a priest, a symposium moderator or a parent educator? How might one give priority to the young children at the beginning of the seder (with skits, quizzes and prizes) and yet raise the adult level of intellectual stimulation later on? Who, on the guest list, are the most promising allies in preparing the seder and what sections of this Haggadah might one send them ahead of time in order to prepare their part?

Please do not be daunted by the enormity of the mission. Remember what Rabbi Tarfon used to say: *"It is not your duty to finish the whole job. But neither are you free from the obligation to engage in the task at hand."* (PIRKEI AVOT 2:16) Do not be intimidated by the size of this Haggadah for it is a **resource book**. It is to be tasted a bit at a time over years to come as you grow and change in your role as leaders of the seder, for you are the most essential link in the innovative tradition of the seder.

A Note on Transliteration

Consonants

All consonants are pronounced as in English except "ch" which is a guttural sound sometimes spelled "kh."

Vowels

a — "ah" like *ma, pa*

ei — "ay" like *day*

i — "i" like *it*

e — "eh" like *bet, set*

ee — long "ē" like *feet*

o — "oh" like *show*

u — "oo" like *fool, pool*

oy — "oy" like *toy*

Chapter 2
The "Jazz" Haggadah

2

The leader of the seder is similar to the conductor of an orchestra and the Haggadah is the musical score. What is the appropriate relationship of the maestro to the masterpiece to be played? How much freedom should be allowed in adapting the music to the audience's needs? Is the Pesach seder meant to be a jam session or a Bach fugue?

In reading the following reflections on contemporary music, we found a succinct statement of the spirit of our Haggadah and of the original Rabbinic seder:

"There has been a general tendency to passivity on the part of the people as an audience for art; they have been receptacles for works developed by others — the artists. A form of specialization emerged — specialization in all the fields. Over the centuries artists have become specialists for the people. They expressed the highest and deepest felt essences of a culture; they painted for the people, they made music for the people, they built buildings for the people. This created a dichotomy whose results are all around us. **A dichotomy between the act of art and the act of life; between the score-maker and the scored-for; between the technician and the layman. It is a dichotomy which did not exist in traditional cultures where all the people were artists, nor does it even now exist among children.**

"In the realm of music, a score can either control or allow leeway. The difference, however, is enormous. In the older music, scoring devices were used to control, with precision, the notes and true intervals played by the performer. **A *Bach score* is Bach and not something else. It communicates exactly what Bach had in mind and controls what the performer does.**

"The newer musical scores on the other hand are not devices for control in the same way. They communicate an idea and a quality — what emerges is something both more and less than what was intended. The hand of the composer lies less heavily on the performer.

"It is the performers almost more than the composer now

who make the music (an approach, incidentally, dating at least back to the beginning of jazz). The inevitable question that arises is: Which is better, that the composer control what we do or that we ourselves play a major role in determining our own music? Each performer must determine this answer for her or himself.

"We are searching for ways to break down this dichotomy, for ways to allow people to enter into the act of making art, as part of the art process of open ended scoring devices which will act as guides, not dictators. These kinds of scores have the built-in possibilities for interaction between what is perceived beforehand and what emerges during the act. **They allow the *activity* itself to generate its own results in process. They communicate but do not control. They energize and guide, they encourage, they evoke responses, they do not impose."**

(LAWRENCE HALPRIN, "*RSVP CYCLES*")

As editors of **A Different Night** we sought to help reverse the trend over the last century that transferred the responsibility for Jewish living from the ordinary Jew to the professional clergy and educators. Choirs, cantors, rabbis and Hebrew educators became our ritual surrogates, while we became "laypeople" in terminology borrowed from the Catholic distinction of priest and laity. In the spirit of the movements represented by the *Jewish Catalog*, the havurah, Jewish camping and the spread of adult Jewish learning, we now seek to return the rituals and the texts to the family leaders who will adapt them to their own spiritual needs.

~ Chapter 3
Preparing for Seder Night:
A Practical Manual

The Overview

The seder night renews annually our connection to Jewish history and its deepest spiritual themes. On this night the generations come together to connect each Jew to the extended family and the whole people, the present to the past and the future. The rescued one is reconnected to the Divine Redeemer and the human being in exile, to a spiritual homeland. The renewal of all these networks takes place in a **common space**, the home, and in **common activities**, the retelling and the reliving of an ancient story.

To achieve these complex goals, the seder needs careful preparation. The greatest error would be to exhaust oneself in cleaning and cooking, in buying and preparing the holiday foods, and then engage in a routine and uninspiring recitation of the Haggadah. Our participatory Haggadah requires that effort be expended beforehand in order to ensure that the seder is innovative and stimulating, and that each participant makes a unique contribution.

The well-prepared seder should look like a jam session, not a pre-scripted concert. The leader is a band leader who guides the group in a certain direction — allowing and encouraging the others to take center stage in turn, with their own variations on the theme. This introduction is designed to help set the stage for your improvisations. Based on the experience of many successful seders, we offer you some suggestions for how and what to prepare in advance in order to ensure that the seder maximizes its potential.

Choosing the Guests

A crucial issue determining the character of any seder is "Who are the participants?" To some extent, this factor is an unalterable given: the immediate family with children of various ages and grandparents. Generally, family considerations take priority; there is, however, latitude in choosing which friends and often which distant relatives to invite. The host family should consider the personality and compatibility of the guests and their ability to enhance the type of participatory seder you intend. One should look both for guests with religious and scholarly background and for people possessing a sense of spontaneity, perhaps a flair for drama or playful creativity. They are the catalysts for setting the tone.

Inviting some guests whom we previously did not know well, or even total strangers, can often contribute to the sense of newness at the seder. An immigrant family from Eastern Europe, or non-Jewish friends or relatives can often provide a sense of spontaneous curiosity about the evening and a sense of cultural contrast which can enliven discussion and pose new and stimulating questions. (Incidentally, there is no halachic problem with inviting non-Jews to share the Pesach meal since there is no Pesach sacrifice without the Temple.)

Whoever is invited can be transformed into an active, willing participant by a simple technique. When inviting the guests, give them an **assignment** in order to enhance their sense of involvement. Ask them to prepare a certain activity or discussion for a particular section of the Haggadah (e.g. "the four children" or "the ten plagues"), and send them copies of the appropriate pages from this Haggadah. Preparation in advance by a variety of participants will give them a sense of ownership and create natural allies for the leader's own innovations. Ask them to limit their presentation to five minutes or less, so that the seder does not become too long.

Involving Non-Jewish Guests

Since the days of Jethro (Yitro) non-Jews have had a special relationship to the Exodus.

"Moses then recounted to his father-in-law everything that the Lord had done to Pharaoh and to the Egyptians for Israel's sake, all the hardships that had befallen them on the way, and how the Lord had delivered them. Then Jethro said, 'Blessed be the Lord who delivered you from the Egyptians and from Pharaoh, and who delivered the people from under the hand of the Egyptians.'"   (EXODUS 18:8-12)

Therefore, like Moses' non-Jewish father-in-law, non-Jews may contribute to the seder.

However, a certain type of involvement should be considered inappropriate. Christian interpretations of the seder as the Last Supper are clearly contradictory to this Jewish holiday of national redemption. A non-Jewish guest who uses the seder to preach the belief in Jesus is at the least impolite and at most reminds Jews of the history of Christian efforts to missionize to Jews or to persecute them, particularly around Easter.

Nonetheless, non-Jews may certainly sing the Psalms and other songs as well as partake in the discussions and eat the symbolic foods. Remembering Pharaoh's daughter who saved baby Moses from being drowned in the Nile, we owe righteous gentiles thanks, especially on Passover.

(See "The Seder of the Righteous Gentile," page 49 of **The Leader's Guide**.)

Making a Festive Atmosphere: Gift Giving

According to the Rabbis, the Biblical injunction "You shall rejoice in your festivals," meant that people should give and receive presents — each one appropriate to his or her tastes. Preparing small personal gifts for the guests and distributing them at the beginning of the seder evening adds a special festive touch. Some families hide the token gifts under the matza cover and distribute them when saying *Ha Lachma Anya* (p. 36).

The Rabbis also ask us to remember the needy on holidays. Jewish communities traditionally collect money (**Maot Chittim**) before Pesach to ensure that no one should lack the necessities for seder night. It is best to enter the seder night with the feeling that you have done your utmost to make sure that no Jew in your community is forced to spend seder night with a sense of want, loneliness or abandonment. Inclusiveness of all the family members and all our people is the watchword of Pesach. Beyond the Jewish community there are the starving and homeless of the world whom the Rabbis command us to

support, for we too were poverty-stricken and persecuted in the land of Egypt and "we know the heart of the stranger."

You may wish to consider the following North American tzedakah funds that specialize in personalized aid to needy individuals:

- **ZIV:** 384 Wyoming Ave., Milburn, NJ 07041. Fax (201) 275-0346. Danny Siegel and Naomi Eisenberg. *or*
- **MAZON: A Jewish Response to Hunger**, 12401 Wilshire Blvd. #303, Los Angeles, CA. 90025. Fax : (310) 442-0030. Irving Cramer.

Helping the Poor: A Story

Once just before Pesach someone arrived at the house of Rabbi Josef-Baer from Brisk, to ask a legal question:

The Questioner: Teach me, Rabbi; can one say Kiddush on Pesach over four cups of milk?

The Rabbi: Pray tell, are you perhaps ill?

The Questioner: No! Thank God, I'm physically well, but (he added in a low voice) wine is a little expensive for me this year.

The Rabbi *to his wife, the Rebbetzin:* Give that man 25 rubles for four cups of wine.

The Questioner: But, Rabbi, I came to ask a question not to request a handout, God forbid.

The Rabbi: This is only a loan until God blesses you with greater prosperity.

The Narrator: After the man had taken the money and gone, the rebbetzin raised a question.

The Rebbetzin: Why did you have to give him 25 rubles? Four cups of wine cannot cost more than two or three rubles.

The Rabbi: You heard his question. He intended to drink four cups of milk at the seder. Surely if he had the funds to eat meat at a complete seder then he could not have drunk milk with his meat meal. I read between the lines of his request and realized that he needed money for all the seder expenses.

Clearing a Space: Cleaning House

An outsider observing a traditional Jewish home during the weeks before Pesach might conclude that the people in the house were not quite sane. They behave like compulsive paranoids — scrubbing, cleaning, dusting and rearranging, all so that no speck of that elusive and mysterious material, "chametz," should remain. Perhaps this impression is not far from the mark! We must realize, however, that this turning of the house, and especially the kitchen, inside out is not a mere "spring cleaning," but an important preparation for the climax of this home-based spiritual celebration — the seder night.

In Egypt the first Pesach was celebrated in the home — the Jewish people ate their Pesach lamb with fear of the plague raging outside their doors and with anticipation of the departure to freedom on the morrow. They prepared the Pesach lamb and dabbed its blood on the doorposts, a life-saving ritual. At the contemporary seder, the home also becomes a sort of **miniature temple** in which the supreme religious act, the telling of the Exodus and the eating of the matza, will take place. There must be a sanctification, a clear separation of the home from its mundane status. In this way we "clear a space for holiness," we remove the every-day and make room for the festive and the sacred.

Traditionally, any place where bread or baked products might be eaten or carried should be swept out. The dishes used year-long have absorbed the taste of leaven-products and are usually replaced by special Passover dishes and tableware or else kashered ones. (The details of kashering are too complex for discussion here and in all doubtful cases, you should consult your local rabbis.)

A Legal Loophole: Selling the Chametz

Local rabbis take care of selling to non-Jews the leaven products which cannot be consumed before Pesach. Thus, one can observe the Biblical injunction that during the whole Pesach holiday, chametz "should be neither seen in the home nor be in one's possession."

Faced with the destruction of significant stores of chametz (such as the cases of whiskey owned by the many Jewish tavern owners in Eastern Europe), the rabbis permitted the sale of the chametz and its products to non-Jews. The rabbis often bent legal rulings about destroying the chametz because of the principle that *"the Torah is concerned to protect Israel's financial resources."* Though, in principle, the sale must be final, in fact the Jew and the non-Jew had a tacit agreement that the sale of the chametz was only for the length of the holiday.

Every year there are new anecdotes about the purchaser — a non-Jew who did not realize that the sale was a legal fiction. Once during Pesach a non-Jewish purchaser came to the Jew's house to claim "his" chametz which was stored in the basement. The Jew had to agree. Recently in the State of Israel whose chief rabbinate sells all the chametz in the country to one non-Jew, there was a scandal. It turned out that the non-Jew had a maternal Jewish grandmother, so he was technically a Jew himself. (For those who dislike legal loopholes, it is preferable simply to remove all the chametz from their homes.)

Preparing the Communal Meal

Seating Arrangements

As at any affair, the seating plan requires some planning in advance. It might be a good idea to seat the younger children at one end of the table in order to busy them with appropriate activities while the adults engage in more serious discussion. Others might give priority to having whole nuclear families seated either side by side or opposite one another, so that the parents can tell the story to their children. Decide which solution is most appropriate for you this year.

A special feature of the seder is **reclining** while drinking wine or eating matza, in imitation of the **dining habits of the nobility** of the Greco-Roman world. Thus in many houses the participants receive a **pillow** to lean back and recline. Children are usually especially enthusiastic about this law. If you request that your guests bring their own pillows, you will enhance the sense that this indeed will be "a different night."

Seder in the Living Room?

Since the usual seder is quite long and seating at the table may be crowded and uncomfortable, some families conduct the first half of their seder (up until the eating of matza and maror) in the lounge or living room. Stretching out on couches arranged in a circle recaptures the original symposium-like atmosphere of the Rabbinic seder. Drinking wine and eating hors d'oeuvres (dipping vegetables) does not require a central table. Storytelling and family dramatic presentations flow easily in this setting.

Still the leader must establish a clear presence and pick a seat with excellent visibility in order to balance the freedom of the living room with the order of the Haggadah.

Setting the Table

As appropriate for a banquet of freedom, the best Passover dishes and tableware should be used. The children may be encouraged to provide colorful placemats as well as to play with toys with holiday themes. Name cards with Hebrew and English names can be prepared to indicate each person's place at the table.

The Seder Plate — One or Many?

Although one could do the minimum[1] and prepare only one central seder plate for the leader, educationally it is preferable to have a seder plate before every three or four participants. Each family invited can bring its own seder plate or the children can prepare homemade plates. These seder plates should contain enough matza, charoset, maror and karpas (whether celery, parsley, or potato) to feed those sitting before it. Many seder plates also increase the number of afikomans being hidden, so that many children can find them and earn prizes.

Matza — Plain, Onion or "Sh'mura"?

The matza must be unleavened. In the preparation of matza the flour is guarded lest it get wet and begin to rise by itself. The usual machine-made matza is supervised from the moment the wheat is ground or the moment it is kneaded. For the very stringent, "matza sh'mura" can be used. This matza is "guarded" from the time the wheat is harvested, hence its name "shmura" — guarded. Onion, egg and chocolate-covered matza are unleavened and they make wonderful treats during Pesach, but are inappropriate at the formal seder when matza represents the unenriched bread of poverty.

Roasted Bone and Egg

On Pesach in the Temple, two sacrifices were offered — the Pesach lamb and the usual holiday sacrifice.[2] The Rabbis commemorated them with **two cooked dishes**, the bone (symbolizing the Pesach sacrifice) and the egg (symbolizing the festival offering). Generally, these are roasted on an open flame just as the Pesach lamb was roasted in Egypt in order to speed the preparation for the departure from slavery. An interesting custom going back to Rav Sherira Gaon (10th C., Babylonia)

involves three cooked dishes on the seder plate: the usual roasted meat and egg along with fish. These three represent Miriam, Aaron and Moses, the siblings whose collective leadership led the people to freedom. (It is not recorded which symbolic food stood for which leader).[3]

What type of bone should be chosen?

Ashkenazim generally avoid using a lamb bone and do not serve mutton or lamb chops on Pesach night lest someone think that this counts as an actual Temple sacrifice. For the same reason, the roasted bone and the roasted egg — unlike the matza, charoset, karpas and maror — are not eaten from the seder plate. Yet some Sefardim do prepare roasted lamb on Pesach as the main course.

What are the customs associated with eggs?

While the roasted egg is a symbol of the holiday sacrifice, boiled eggs are often eaten at the seder because they symbolize the circle of life and death. The mournful symbolism is related to the fact that the Temple has been destroyed and no actual Pesach sacrifices may be offered.

Charoset

The preparation of charoset — by chopping and mixing and beating — is itself part of the process of remembering the preparation in Egypt of mud bricks with straw. Recipes vary and as suggested in our Haggadah (page 127), it is fun to taste and compare recipes and to let the guests guess at the original ingredients, while at the seder itself. On the next page are three traditional recipes mandated by the rabbis.

Recipes vary throughout the world. The key is to include:

☛ Fruits and nuts mentioned in the Song of Songs, sung on Pesach, which are identified with the people of Israel: 1) pomegranates, 2) apples, 3) figs, 4) dates, 5) walnuts, 6) chestnuts, 7) almonds, 8) raisins, 9) sweet wine.

☛ Pungent spices to recall the straw used to reinforce the mud bricks in Egypt: 10) pepper, 11) ginger, 12) cumin, 13) cinnamon sticks, 14) celery. (Some add pears to simulate the color of mortar, and bananas to add the viscosity of mortar.)

☛ A sharp distasteful liquid to recall the pungent taste of slavery: 15) vinegar, 16) dry wine.

☛ A process of preparation similar to brick-making involving mashing and kneading, as with mortar and pestle.[4]

Recipe #1:

Rabbi Isaac Luria (KABBALIST, TZEFAT, 16TH C)

Seven chopped fruits and nuts mentioned in the Song of Songs, like walnuts, figs, and pomegranates, grapes, apples, pears and dates. Three spices like ginger, cinnamon sticks, and sweet spike nard. (In Northern Europe where many fruits were unavailable in the spring, Jews simply used walnuts, apples and pears).

Recipe #2:

Maimonides (TALMUDIST, PHILOSOPHER, EGYPT, 12TH C)

Figs and dates are soaked and then cooked. Then they are mashed and mixed with vinegar, straw-like grasses (like celery), and the spice "nard."[5]

Recipe #3:

Rabbi Kapach (YEMENITE, ISRAEL, 20TH C)

Charoset is called "*Dukeh*," meaning smashed fruits and nuts: dates (300 grams), raisins (300 g), figs (100 g), sesame (200 g), pomegranate (1), almonds (100 g), walnuts (100 g), black pepper (20 g), cumin (20 g), cinnamon sticks (10 g), zangwill (ginger) (10 g).

Karpas — Celery and Assorted Dips: An Expanded Smorgasbord

Though legally a minimum of celery is adequate for dipping, we highly recommend offering diversified and plentiful **hors d'oeuvres**. These finger foods should be available right after the eating of the **karpas** with salt water. Each appetizer should be served with its characteristic dip.

For example: celery in salt water • gefilte fish in horseradish • artichoke in mayonnaise • potato chips in ketchup • hard boiled eggs in salt water • carrots in guacamole • boiled potatoes in salt water.

The expanded dipping is probably an innovation for most family seders, but it is mandated for several pressing reasons — pragmatic, educational, historical and symbolic.

a. Pragmatic: People are hungry especially after a long day of pre-seder preparations without bread or matza meals. Daylight savings time often postpones the beginning of the seder which traditionally does not begin before sundown. People often have a Pavlovian response to sitting at a table, therefore finding it difficult to sit for an hour's discussion without eating anything but a piece of celery. Rabbi Joel Sirkis sums up the point: **"We dip now before the meal, because we cannot wait so long without eating anything. In fact, people generally dip before a meal in order to whet their appetites, though they should not fill their stomachs completely."** (17TH C. POLAND)

b. Educational: Lengthy storytelling and discussions during the Maggid, the heart of the Haggadah, cannot easily be done properly on an empty stomach. Moreover, the very novelty of introducing varied dips will arouse child and adult alike to ask: Why is this night different than all other (seder) nights? Why do we dip vegetables before we eat? To arouse curiosity is precisely the explanation given for the dipping of *karpas* in the Talmud.[6]

c. Historical: This expanded *"karpas"* reflects the original form of symposia and rabbinic meals including the seder. In the earliest Haggadah (9TH C., BABYLONIA) Rav Amram Gaon states: **"various vegetables are served like lettuce or celery or kusbara, etc."** The Cairo Genizah preserves an early medieval hagaddah from Eretz Yisrael with blessings for dipping that include vegetables, fruits and even rice mixed with eggs and honey.[7]

These dips betoken the lifestyle of the upper class citizens of Greece and Rome for whom drinking cocktails and especially dipping a wide assortment of vegetables was a distinctive mark of high class living. Especially in an era before refrigeration and supermarkets, fresh vegetables were reserved for persons of means. *"The Caesar and Rabbi Yehuda HaNasi, head of the Sanhedrin, were so rich that their table never lacked for turnips, for* chazeret *(horseradish), or for squash, neither in summer nor in winter."*[8]

Maror and Chazeret — Lettuce or Horseradish?

The rabbis gave preference to Romaine lettuce as **maror**, but Eastern European Jews, whose spring came late, generally used the much stronger maror — horseradish (*chrein*).

Most seder plates have two places for bitter herbs, for *maror* and for *chazeret* (a sharp, spicy condiment), but the obligation is only to eat *maror*, whether as lettuce or as horseradish. For many, it is customary to use Romaine lettuce for *maror* and to place ground or sliced, red or white horseradish on the seder plate, where it says *chazeret*.

The amount of lettuce or horseradish to be prepared should reflect the requirement that approximately one ounce (29 grams) of maror be eaten both by itself and again as part of the Hillel Sandwich.

Nuts, Raisins and Candy on the Seder Plate?

Rabbi Akiva used to rush home from the House of Study on Pesach evening **"to distribute toasted grain (popcorn?) and nuts to the children to keep them from falling asleep and to arouse their curiosity to ask questions."** [9] Therefore, some medieval Jews used to put "toasted grains, nuts, sweets and fruits on the seder plate in order to coax the children to stay awake and to arouse inquiry." [10] It is probably a great idea! Even if there is no room on the fancy seder plate, a basket of treats placed next to the seder plate and distributed ostentatiously just before the four questions will serve the same educational function of providing surprise and delight.

Afikoman Envelopes

The afikoman — the larger half of the middle matza — is usually wrapped in a napkin and hidden. The napkin symbolizes the clothing of the Jews who wrapped the dough in their garments on their shoulders when they were chased out of Egypt. An embroidered afikoman envelope, a nice pillow case, or at least a decorative napkin can be prepared in advance. This prevents crumbs, makes the afikoman more easily identifiable and offers another occasion to use art to enhance the mitzvah.

Two Types of Seder Plate

Most ceramic seder plates are produced in the Hassidic and Sefardic tradition of HaAri, Rabbi Isaac Luria, the Kabbalist (16th C., Tzefat, Eretz Yisrael).

The location of the symbolic foods reflects the 10 *sefirot*, emanations of the Divine, according to Jewish mysticism: 6 foods on the plate, 3 matzot, and 1 seder plate.

Nevertheless, these customs regarding the seder plate are not so rigid. Often the three matzot are placed separately in a basket or three-tiered cloth cover next to the seder plate rather than under it, so that they are accessible and not easily broken. Some Yemenites have no seder plate at all. The table itself is filled with

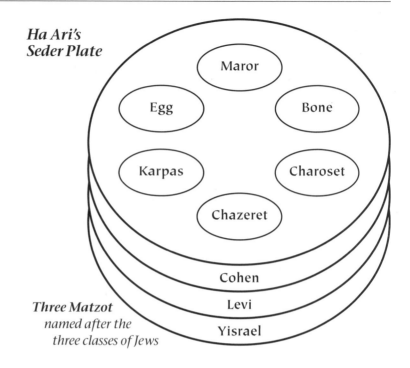

Ha Ari's Seder Plate

Maror
Egg   Bone
Karpas   Charoset
Chazeret
Cohen
Levi
Yisrael

Three Matzot named after the three classes of Jews

the various symbolic foods.

It is interesting to note an alternative tradition of Lithuanian scholars following the Vilna Gaon. Basing himself on Maimonides' rulings, the Vilna Gaon used a three-tiered seder plate:

Top: **Charoset** (left) and **Maror** (right)

Middle: **Two Matzot** covered with a cloth

Bottom: **Egg** (left) and **Bone** (right)

Wine

Prepare enough wine or grape juice for each participant (four cups apiece). This should be the best quality wine. The rabbis preferred red wine, though it need not be sweet.

Music of the Haggadah

Singing is important for any social gathering — especially one with children. Traditionally the main songs are the *Kiddush*, *Hallel* (the Psalms), and *Da-yeinu* before the meal and more *Hallel* and table songs like *Chad Gadya* at the end. In *A Different Night*, most songs as well as blessings are transliterated so everyone can sing along. It also includes many other songs — both traditional as well as American freedom songs. In the section on the Ten Plagues we include "Let My People Go" and "If I Had A Hammer." After the meal we include Elijah songs, *Hatikva*, the Jewish national anthem, and "Down by the Riverside."

Unfortunately, many of us do not know the traditional melodies. Tapes of Pesach songs are available at Jewish bookstores. Someone with musical ability can be assigned to learn and to teach these songs. Alternatively you can sing the Hebrew words (for example, *Chad Gadya*) to English language melodies like "There was an old lady who swallowed a fly."

Dressing Up: as a Priest or a Refugee or as Elijah the Prophet

Obviously, one dresses up both to create a festive atmosphere and to celebrate our elevated status as free beings. The leader of the seder may also wear a long, white "*kittel*" — an elegant white robe — to imitate the high priest.[11]

In addition, children can be provided with dress up clothes. At *Yachatz* when the matza is broken in two, and when *ha lachma anya* is said, it is customary for the children, dressed in old clothes, to appear at the door. They carry matza on their shoulders wrapped in cloth (or in a backpack) and imitate the Jewish refugees on their way from Egypt to Jerusalem.

After the meal when the cup of Elijah is poured, some families assign someone to dress as Elijah and wait outside the door, entering when it is opened to recite *Sh'foch chamatcha* (see p. 142). This custom is reported in medieval Europe by an apostate Jew named Antonius Margaritha (1530): *"At the moment when the door is opened someone dressed in costume quickly enters the room as if he were Elijah the Prophet himself. It is as if the prophet has come to announce the coming of the Jews' Messiah."*[12] In preparing to impersonate Elijah, remember that he used to dress in a long fur coat and he had long, wild hair. *(II KINGS 1:8, 2:8)*

Special Customs of the Day of the Seder:

The Fast of the First-Born

From morning until nightfall on the day of the seder, it is customary, though not obligatory, for the first-born of the family to refrain from eating or drinking. The first-borns recall that had they been in Egypt their lives would have hung in the balance with the Plague of the First-Born. Who is considered a first-born? There are three views: (1) the first male fruit of the mother's womb *(EXODUS 13:1-2, 14-15)*, (2) the first-born male of father or mother,[13] (3) the first-born whether male or female.[14] Generally, first-borns attend a celebration on the morning before Pesach which takes precedence over the fast. For example, they join someone marking the completion of a Torah study cycle and turn the would-be fast into a feast. Some rabbis regret this rampant use of a legal fiction to undermine the fast.

No More Chametz

From approximately 10 A.M. Jewish law does not permit the eating of chametz products. At this time the remains of the chametz are burned. *(See details on pages 14-15 of the haggadah).*

No Sneak-previews of the Matza!

It is quite a challenge to work up an appetite for matza — so dry and plain, truly a bread of poverty. In addition, the Rabbis wanted the eating of matza at the seder to be truly special, set off from the eating of matza which might take place at any time during the year. Therefore, the Rabbis forbade the eating of matza on the day of the seder. At the afternoon meal before the seder, when chametz is already forbidden, but matza not yet permitted, one may eat meat, vegetables or potatoes. Note that **egg matza** is not appropriate for fulfilling the mitzvah of eating matza on seder night — but it is permitted to be eaten on the day of the seder. Many people avoid eating any kind of matza for several weeks before the seder.

Unlike Shabbat and other holidays when we eat shortly after nightfall, on Pesach we relate at length the story of the Exodus before enjoying the festive meal. In order to prevent hunger and its attending sense of impatience from interfering with our storytelling, it is wise to eat a light meal about an hour before sundown.

Perhaps a Short Nap?

Parents often worry about the kids being able to stay awake until the end of the seder. They may require that the kids nap beforehand. Isn't it equally important that the parents sit down to the seder rested and alert? Good planning before the seder should include a short nap for the adults, and especially the hosts of the evening.

Chapter 4
Young Children at the Seder:
Age-Appropriate Activities

4

The seder is a highly structured activity with participants of many ages, representing multiple generations. Each person comes to the seder with his or her own set of expectations and experiences of previous family seders. It would be wise to consider each participant's expected attention span for the evening's program. Some school-age children may surprise the adults by their enthusiastic participation.

The following section serves to guide those preparing for the seder which is attended by young children. Several of the suggested activities can be performed at the child's home in advance of the seder; some of the arts and crafts work are to be taken to the seder itself and subsequently used. Our list also includes many impromptu activities for the evening itself.

Depending on the age spread and the children's knowledge and previous involvement with the seder it could be arranged to set-up a "Pesach Play room" at the home of the seder. This will give the younger children a place to spend some very special time when the seder itself becomes too cumbersome for them. We suggest creating activity centers adjacent to the seder table or in an adjoining room. Children of all ages can spend time here before the long sit-down seder begins while the adults are busy making last-minute arrangements. Alternatively, the younger participants can have their own Pesach educational activities in their Pesach Play room, while the majority of the adults and teenagers participate in the more serious symposium-like aspects of the Haggadah beginning some time after the Four Questions. Setting up a special area for your children may inspire them to ask that most important question: "What is the difference between this night and all other nights?"

Pesach Play Room Suggestions:

• **Impromptu Dramatics:** Transform the room into a stage set for the story of baby Moshe, for the adult Moshe's confronta-

tion with Pharaoh or for the ten plagues. Provide dress and props, such a gowns, crowns, snakes, staffs, throne, wicker basket and ten plagues. Children and parents could research illustrated books on ancient Egypt and the descriptions in the book of Exodus so all the props are authentic to the time period. Arts and crafts projects (before the seder) can enhance the Oscar-winning costume design of the entire family.

• **Book Display and Story Reading:** Ask each guest to bring illustrated Bible books of the Exodus and display them on a table. The early arriving guests can read stories to the children and point out the different versions of the same story and the variety of illustrations of the same topic.

• **Storytelling with Puppets:** Sock puppets, paper cutouts pasted to popsicle sticks, brown paper bag puppets provide hours of fun preparation before the seder and many more hours of high drama during the seder as Moshe, Miriam, Aaron, Pharaoh and some of the Ten Plagues walk on stage. Stretch a sheet across the room at waist level and ask parents and children to create the dialogue as they display the puppets above the stage line of the sheet for the rest of the guests.

• **Building Egypt and the Exodus:** Just about every household with children features a collection of building blocks, Lego, Duplo, and small figurines. Children of every age delight in building their version of the story as it is told to them by their older siblings, their parents or grandparents. Buildings could stay on display for several days after the seder so as to add afterwards the splitting of the Red Sea on the last day of Pesach.

• **Audio-visual presentations:** In recent years a wealth of children's audio and video tapes on the Jewish Holidays have been made available through the local Jewish bookstores and the synagogue giftshops. Listening and viewing educational shows is a nice quiet activity before the holiday starts and during the hours before the seder gets on its way.

Crafts Projects:

• Haggadah bookmarks

• The child's own Haggadah

• Mobiles with Pesach symbols (such as matza, wine cups, Elijah's beaker, maror), Pesach figures (such as Moshe, Miriam, Pharaoh and Pharaoh's daughter) or paper cut-outs of the child's own family present at the seder

• Paper bag dramatics, hand puppets

• Matza covers and pillow cases for reclining, made from a variety of textiles

• Coloring books, fold-out books

• "Welcome to our seder" door signs

• Place cards for each guest at the seder. The cards could be written in English as well as featuring the person's Hebrew name.

• Prompting cards for the various sections of the seder to be displayed on a large board.

Card Games (to be prepared in advance):

You may ask an older child or a talented parent to prepare these simple games for the seder night.

• **Memory:** Cards with a picture of a seder object or activity that match an identical picture or the name of that object, either in English or in Hebrew (for example: the word "Afikoman" and a picture of a hidden matza on a matching card).

• **Put in order:** Cards for each of the 15 activities on the seder agenda (Kadesh, Urchatz) that must be put in order.

• **Quartet**s: Use four differently colored sets of cards. Each set consists of four items of the seder agenda (the four cups, the four children, the four questions, four foods on the seder plate, four names for Pesach).

• **Seder means "Order:"** The children can help mark the progress of the seder for everyone. Prepare a large tag board entitled "Seder." At the beginning of the seder, distribute cards to the children with Hebrew, English and picture names of the key signposts of the evening. For example, use the names of ritual activities (kadesh/first cup; urchatz/hand washing) or key texts of the Haggadah (four questions/ma nishtana) listed in the table of contents. As each activity or text is reached, the leader calls on the three holders of the English, Hebrew and the pictorial name card to attach them to the tag board (by Velcro

or large paper clips).

• **Questions for everyone at *Ma Nishtana*:** School age children will enjoy quizzing the older children and the parents in the following way. Prepare index cards with Pesach questions on one side and the answers on the other. Each child chooses a partner to whom s/he poses the questions. For example: "I am made from chopped nuts, apples and wine. Who am I?"/ "Charoset." Questions can be posed on many different levels of difficulty, depending on the participants' age, knowledge and curiosity. Each question earns the child one nut or candy if answered correctly and two if the adult is stumped. Adults may also buy hints from the child for nuts or candy.

• **Open ended questions on cards:** It is even more interesting to pose open ended questions such as: "When you were a slave in Egypt, what was the most unpleasant part of your life?" or "What was your favorite memory as a child from the seder?" "What is your favorite seder song?" "Which one of the ten plagues is the worst for you?"

Quizzes:

Asking questions is a time-honored activity among Jewish families, so here at the seder we add some more action to *Ma Nishtana*. Parents, grandparents, teachers, seder guests can all prepare in advance various forms of quizzes for the younger ones. Even an adult quiz will be a welcome addition to the seder.

• **Who Said to Whom** from the story of Exodus (chapters 1-12).

• **Word Scrambles:** For example: SAPEHC, S'LEIAHJ PCU.

• **Charades** of the Ten Plagues.

• **Passover Mathematics:** For example: how much are The Plagues (10) times The Cups (4) minus the Matzot (3).

• **Pesach Trivia** in teams with points. Teams can be comprised of families, age mates, left side of table against right side.

• **Chametz or Not:** Make a list of difficult items such a spaghetti, beer, noodles, crackers, potato chips, latkes, hamantashen, kneidlach, muffins, lasagna, whiskey, blintzes, pancakes, kreplach. Each correct answer receives a point, each incorrect answer receives a promise to receive that food as a gift after Pesach.

• **Guess Who I Am:** Place a headband on each participant's head with a slot for a word like Moshe, *matza*, frogs, locust, *chad gadyah, dayenu*. Only the person him/herself does not know who or what is written. By asking "yes"/"no" questions each one guesses their own identity.

• **Cross word puzzles** prepared at various levels of difficulty.

Nutty Games:

Since nuts are a traditional food on Pesach, many regular games and sports can feature nuts instead of the usual coins, peons or dice. Special concern should be taken that the smaller children are not endangered by eating nuts; they can be compensated by special Pesach foods.

Games that can be played with nuts are:

• Pitch nuts into boxes or "pyramids" with various values.

• Hide nuts in bunches throughout the house. Before the nuts can be eaten, the children have to answer questions, perform a small task or sing a song.

• Nuts can be given as prizes for answering the quizzes correctly or for helping the parents in preparing for the seder.

"Plastering Pharaoh:" The Ten Plagues Revisited:

At children's stores buy stickers or plastic representations of frogs, wild animals, insects, darkness, etc. for each one of the ten plagues. Distribute the plagues to the children and prepare a tag board with a large picture of Pharaoh. As each plague is read off during the seder, invite one child to "plaster" Pharaoh with the appropriate stickers or tape on the plastic figures or by throwing Ping-Pong balls (hail) at Pharaoh. Traditional religious observance does not permit the use of tape on a holiday, therefore this activity is appropriate before the seder starts.

Relay Storytelling for Older Children and Adults:

Begin telling the story of Exodus, embellishing as you go, then stop and hand the "baton" or "matza" on to the next storyteller to continue where you left off.

Adapted Shows with Pesach Topics:

• Concentration
• What's My Line
• Password
• Meet The Press
• Jeopardy (guess the question from the answer)
• To Tell The Truth.

Resources for Children:

When you get ready to plan your children's participation at this year's seder, you should consider using the following resources:

• Visit your local Jewish book store, the synagogue gift shop and contact the Bureau of Jewish Education in your community.

• You can order directly from publishers such as Kar-Ben, Torah Aura, Alternatives in Religious Education, Behrman House, the Melton Center at JTSA (Conservative), CCAR (Reform) or Artscroll (Orthodox).

• In case you have family in Israel, you can ask them to send you the latest audio- and video tapes, stickers, workbooks and kits for crafts projects.

• Consult with your child's JCC pre-school staff, Hebrew School or Day School teachers. How did the children prepare for Pesach at school, which projects did they participate in, how can the home enhance the learning at school?

Passover Word Square

In the HEBREW month of NISSAN, at the PASSOVER SEDER, we read from the HAGGADAH. We recall that the Jews were SLAVES in the land of EGYPT. PHARAOH kept them oppressed and would not heed the word of MOSES to let the people go. PLAGUES were brought down upon the land of Egypt and finally the Jews were ordered to leave. The parting of the RED SEA allowed the Jews to escape the pursuing Egyptians and reach the DESERT. Here they wandered for FORTY years before entering the PROMISED LAND. In retelling the story of the EXODUS, we remind ourselves of the importance of FREEDOM.

Each of the capitalized words can be found in the word square below. Words may appear forwards or backwards, horizontally, vertically, or diagonally. Circle each word as you find it.

```
H A E R A P L A G U E S
E A E X P E O M O S E S
B L G A O T S N I S G E
R E Y G L D L D X Y Y V
E X O Y A P U R E T P A
W O R E S D E S E R T L
P R O M I V A E G U S S
H Y T R O F O H A F E E
A D E S E D E R D S E D
R E S O M O D E E R F R
N A S I N P H A R A O H
P R O M I S E D L A N D
```

Chapter 5
Short Cuts through the Haggadah: How to Pick and Choose

Setting Priorities

The leader's dilemma: "How can I recite all the sections of the traditional Haggadah, add creative activities and discussions, and still get to the meal in a decent interval that doesn't exasperate many of the less patient participants?" For many families the answer will be: you can't! Therefore priorities must be set. In this section we provide guidelines for seder leaders on how to pick and choose; how to recognize the essentials of the seder which must not be dropped or done superficially. We also identify the less essential parts, both in terms of their educational utility and Jewish law (*halacha*), which may be skipped over if necessary.

In order to enable the seder leader to set priorities with a feeling of confidence and familiarity with the material of the Haggadah, this section provides the following:

- A review of the basic four-cup structure of the seder.
- The essential building blocks of the storytelling (*Maggid*) section of the Haggadah.
- A distinguishing of obligatory from optional parts of the Haggadah text from the standpoint of traditional Jewish law.
- Two examples of possible seders: the first, a one-hour "bare-bones-basic," and the second, a longer seder in which educational activities and discussion take the place of some of the less-essential traditional texts.
- A list of recommended activities, readings, and songs which we can choose from and vary at each seder.

Maimonides enjoins us to be creative: "to make a change in the routine on that night" so as to engage actively all the participants in a genuine search for meaning and understanding.

The Four Cups: The Key to the Overall Structure of the Seder

At first glance the traditional Haggadah may seem like a hodge-podge of texts and activities. That first impression is not surprising, for the Haggadah is an eclectic anthology constructed by many hands over two thousand years. Therefore we have brought out the basic structure of the Haggadah built around the four cups which punctuate the four basic sections. Each of the four major sections is keyed on the side of the page by a graphic representation of a cup:

First Cup: "Kiddush"

The evening opens with sanctification of the holiday by an initial invocation.

Second Cup: "Maggid"

Questions and storytelling fill this longest part of the seder. After telling the story of Exodus and explaining the symbolic foods that trigger memories of Egypt, we sing a song of praise to God our liberator.

Third Cup: "Shulchan Orech"

The meal begins with matza and maror and concludes with the long blessing after eating called "Birkat HaMazon."

Elijah's Cup

The opening of the door expresses messianic expectation.

The Fourth Cup: "Hallel"

The psalms and their blessings are sung responsively.

Concluding Songs

The famous medieval folksongs like "Chad Gadya" constitute an appendix to the rabbinic four cup structure.

Maggid

The most important landmarks of the seder from an educational point of view occur within the *Maggid* — the Second Cup devoted to storytelling. Four aspects invite greater depth and enrichment:

1) initiating a questioning process at *Ma Nishtana* / Four Questions (p. 40).

2) retelling the story of the Egyptian Exodus and subsequent exoduses in history and in our lives at *Avadeem Hayeenu* / "We Were Slaves" (p. 44).

3) bridging the generation gap and opening up a dialogue between parents and children at the *Four Children* (p. 56).

4) reflecting philosophically on slavery and freedom at the Rabbinic Midrash *Arami Oved Avi* (p. 81).

We should never try to expand on all four sections of the Haggadah at the same seder, but there should be one evening every few years devoted to each of these facets.

Planning the Itinerary of Your Seder

After reading the User's Guide in the Haggadah (page 4), you will be ready to plan your seder. Your task is twofold:

(1) to select the traditional texts and supplementary readings and activities appropriate for the family and friends who will attend this year's seder; and

(2) to maximize the involvement of others in the seder as well as make it easier on yourself.

Begin by skimming the Table of Contents of **A Different Night**, noting its basic structure built around the Four Cups. Choose a section like the Signposts (the formal opening of the seder) or the *Ma Nishtana* and leaf through the texts and

supplements to familiarize yourself with them. Notice the Bare Bones Basics signified by a colored ❖ symbol.

Now select an appropriate length of time for reading the Haggadah up to the meal. Consider your halachic commitments (traditional Jewish legal obligations). Do you insist on a minimum legal standard or do you use the traditional text as a resource to be shortened or expanded according to your needs?

Below you will find a few **introductory itineraries** through the seder: the Bare Bones Basic Seder; one longer, more creative seder; and the halachic minimal seder. You may wish to use them until you develop your own style and your own favorite pieces.

■ The Bare Bones Basics

The Bare Bones Basics offers a basic structure for a **1 hour** seder before eating and for a recommended **20 minutes** of singing after the meal. The B.B.B. before the meal should take a little over 30 minutes, leaving another 30 minutes or more of enrichment materials. These creative additions can be geared for young kids *(See Chapter 4 — Young Children at the Seder),* for teenagers, or for adults. Generally the children deserve attention in the earlier parts of the seder, but adults are also very important participants who deserve to learn and discuss at more sophisticated levels. A detailed outline of the B.B.B. can be found in the Haggadah itself on page 8.

We suspect you will probably want to vary and expand on the B.B.B., but this is a good way to get started.

■ A Longer, More Creative Seder: A Sample

(approximately 1.5 hours from kiddush to eating)

1. Signposts for the seder: sing *Kaddesh Urchatz,* p. 20

2. First Cup: *Kiddush,* p. 24

3. Reading: From Rags to Riches, p. 27

4. Dips: *Urchatz, Karpas,* p. 30

5. Break Matza: *Yachatz,* p. 32

6. Activity: A Passover Skit, p. 35

7. The Story of the Matza: *Ha Lachma,* p. 36

8. Four Questions: *Ma Nishtana,* p. 40

9. Reading: "Izzy, Did You Ask?" p. 47

10. Storytelling: We were slaves (sing *Avadeem Hayeenu*), p. 44

11. Reading: from "Chronicles: New of the Past," p. 54

12. Four Children: Assign roles and read the text out loud, pp. 56, 58, 60

13. Activity: Compare different depictions of the "four children," pp. 62-71

14. Rav's Story: Spiritual slavery, p. 72

15. The Promise: sing *V'hee She-amda*, p. 76

16. *Arami Oved Avi* — read texts on "The Wandering Jew," p. 78, and do "passport" activity, p. 115
   [Young children prepare for "Yukkiest Plague" skits, p. 97, while older participants discuss one of the symposium topics, p. 81]

17. The Ten Plagues — spill out the drops, p. 98

18. Activity for children — The Yukkiest Plague

19. *Dayeinu:* sing together, p. 104

20. Explain *Pesach, Matza, Maror*, pp. 110-112

21. "In Every Generation," p. 114

22. Reading: Body Language, p. 115

23. *Hallel:* Psalms 113-114, p. 116

24. Second Cup: Blessings of Redemption, p. 122

25. Wash hands, then eat *Matza, Maror,* and *Korech,* pp. 124, 126, 128

26. FESTIVE MEAL

27. Eat *Afikoman,* p. 130

28. Recite or sing *Birkat Ha-Mazon,* p. 132

29. Third Cup, p. 137

30. Elijah's Cup and welcoming songs, p. 138
   Shfoch Cha-mat-cha, p. 142

31. Hallel and its blessings, p. 144

32. Fourth Cup and blessings, p. 149

33. Concluding Songs:
   (1) *Echad Mee Yodei-a,* p. 155
   (2) *Chad Gadya,* p. 160
   (3) Next Year in Jerusalem, p. 165

■ Traditional Jewish Law: Legal Minimums of the Seder*

Reading every paragraph of the traditional Haggadah is not legally obligatory. In fact, if one carefully reads every word, there are still several central legal requirements that will have been ignored. For example, the commandment to **ask** questions is not fulfilled by merely singing *Ma Nishtana*. Children or adults must really inquire, not merely recite. Another example is *Avadeem Ha-yeenu*. The mitzvah is to tell the story of the Exodus in a way appropriate for different levels of interest and intelligence. Merely reading one sentence: "We were slaves" (DEUTERONOMY 6:21) is inadequate. In fact, the Haggadah never offers a script for the storytelling. One has fulfilled the mandate only when the listeners not only know the facts but also feel as if they personally went out of Egypt. Arousing curiosity and creative storytelling are essential halachic requirements not embraced by a rote reading of the text.

The halachic minimum suggested below is an invitation to add more, not to shorten the seder. As the Haggadah recommends, "The more one expands on the story, the more commendable." In case of doubt consult your rabbi. As we all know, there are many views in Jewish law. This is one view. Although many traditional texts are optional, we do **not** necessarily recommend that they be skipped.

1. Candlelighting, p. 16
   • [optional: the poem *Kadesh Urchatz* is merely a medieval poem, p. 20]

2. *Kiddush* and *She-he-chee-yanu*, p. 22
   • [optional: *Hee-ne-nee Muchan*]

3. *Urchatz, Karpas, Yachatz*, p. 28/30/32

4. *Ha Lachma Anya*, p. 36

5. *Ma Nishtana*, p. 40

6. Shmuel's Story: *Avadeem Hayeenu*, p. 44
   • [optional: the rabbis of B'nei Brak and Ben Zoma, p. 46]
   • [optional halachically, but very important: The Midrash of the Four Children, p. 56]

*We are grateful to **Rabbi Yaacov Warhaftig**, director of the Ariel Institute, Orthodox Rabbinical Seminary in Jerusalem, who gave us his advice and approval for this section.

7. Rav's Story: *Mee-Tchee-la,* "Our Ancestors Were Idol Worshippers," p. 72

   • [optional but customary is The Promise and *V'hee She-amda,* p. 76]

8. *Arami Oved Avi,* p. 78

   The obligation is to read and comment in rabbinic style on the entire section from Deuteronomy 26. However, if one enters into a creative symposium on these verses, rather than reading the whole rabbinic midrash (*Sifrei*) word for word, this may be a wholly appropriate fulfillment of the mitzvah. The Ten Plagues, p. 98, are simply the final section of the Midrash on *Arami Oved Avi.*

   • [optional: the midrash on 50, 200, 250 plagues]

   • [optional though very traditional and ancient is *Da-yeinu,* p. 104]

9. Rabban Gamliel: *Pesach, Matza, Maror,* p. 110

10. "In Every Generation" *B'Chol Dor Va'Dor,* p. 114

11. *Hallel* Psalm 113-114, p. 116

12. Second Cup, p. 122

13. Washing hands and Eating *Matza* and *Maror,* and *Korech,* pp. 124/126/128]

14. *Afikoman,* p. 130

15. *Birkat HaMazon,* p. 132

16. Third Cup, p. 137

17. *Sh'foch Cha-mat-cha,* p. 142

18. *Hallel* and its Blessings, p. 144

19. Fourth Cup and the Blessings after it, p. 149

20. *Sefirat HaOmer* is obligatory on the 2nd seder night, p. 159

   • [optional: all the poems and songs including *Nirtza* and Next Year in Jerusalem]

The Top Ten Activities, Readings and Songs in *"A Different Night"*

■ *Activities:*

1. Blessing the Children, p. 18
2. Karpas: Multiple Appetizers, p. 30
3. A Personal Thanksgiving, p. 33
4. A Passover Skit, p. 35
5. Eliciting Questions, p. 41
6. My Most Unusual Seder, p. 47
7. Reading *Chronicles:* News of the Past, p. 54
8. The Contemporary Four Children, p. 61
9. The Artist as Commentator: The Art of the Four Children, p. 62, 175
10. The Afghani Onion Free-for-All, p. 107

■ *Readings and Stories:*

1. From Rags to Riches, p. 27
2. This year we are Slaves, p. 39
3. Izzy, did you ask a good question today? p. 41
4. By Tomorrow, Today will be a Story, I. B. Singer, p. 45
5. A Philosopher at Home, David Hartman, p. 48
6. The Four Parents: Children Label their Parents, p. 57
7. A Rabbi's Memoir of Berlin, 1933-1937, p. 77
8. ZPG: Zero Population Growth, p. 91
9. A Toast to Freedom, p. 117
10. Anne Frank: I Still Believe, p. 141

■ *Songs:*

1. Kadesh UrChatz, p. 20
2. Ma Nishtana, p. 40
3. Da-yeinu, p. 104
4. Freedom Songs, p. 119
5. Elijah's Songs, p. 140
6. Who Knows One / Echad Mee Yodei-a, p. 155
7. Just One Little Kid / Chad Gadya, p. 160
8. Next Year in Jerusalem / L'Shana HaBa-a, p. 165
9. Hatikvah and Jerusalem of Gold, p. 166
10. Down by the Riverside, p. 169

5

PART II
SEDER SUPPLEMENTS

✍ Chapter 6
The Four Questions in Depth

מַה נִּשְׁתַּנָּה

6

Maimonides: How to Activate the 'Spontaneous' Question

Initially we might assume that the unique practices of the seder night themselves would arouse the spontaneous question. The Talmud, however, relates that at many seders the leader would not rely on the ritual differences intrinsic to Pesach, but would initiate other unusual practices "so that the children would inquire." *(BABYLONIAN TALMUD, PESACHIM 108)* Maimonides summarized these Talmudic customs and extrapolated a basic educational principle of the seder night:

> "One must make a change in the seder (routine) on this night so that the children will take note and ask, and say "How different this night is from all other nights!" and the father will answer them and say to them "such and such happened, such and such took place."

> "*How does one make a change? By distributing parched corn or nuts [ancient candy!] or by removing the table before them before they eat, or by snatching things from one another's hands, and similar things.*" (MISHNE-TORAH, LAWS OF MATZA 7:3)

Why the need to initiate new surprises beyond the unique practices of the seder itself? It would seem that dipping celery in salt water and reclining on pillows might intrigue the children the first time they see it. Thereafter it would be recognized as part of the routine of Pesach. The Rabbis introduced further novelties, including "snatching things from one another" (apparently the source of the custom to steal the afikoman and hide it). This reflects an educational strategy in which surprise and questioning are actively pursued by upsetting the expected *"seder"* (which means "order") with anarchic, irreverent play.

We call on those who wish to recapture the genuine questioning spirit of the original Rabbinic seder to follow the lead of Maimonides: The leader of the seder should take a little time and effort before the seder to think up some unusual and surprising actions which will arouse the curiosity of the children and lead them to ask the *genuine* question: Ma-Nishtana? What's going on here? What in the world are you doing? (And *why?*)

Four Ideas to Stimulate Questioning

To get you started thinking — here are a few examples of eyebrow-raising activities in the spirit of the Talmud. The activities should take place immediately following the filling of the second cup of wine, or immediately after the ritual recitation of the Four Questions by the young children.

"Dessert first?"

The leaders of the seder begin to pass out candies or sweets to the children, even though it's long before dessert is to be served. When they ask "What for? What's going on?" the leaders invite them to offer their own explanations. Afterwards one may wish to answer their questions in this spirit:

> Congratulations on showing that you are children "who have intelligence," by taking note of the fact that something unusual is happening. This shows that you have the healthy characteristics of free people. You don't take anything for granted and you insist on understanding what is happening about you.
>
> Now let me explain why I enticed you with sweets. The Rabbis explain that the beginning of Israel's story in Egypt was sweet and only in the end did it become bitter (JERUSALEM TALMUD PESACHIM 2:5). Egypt's glittering civilization seemed attractive to the Israelites who increasingly identified with it. Only later did they become aware of the dangers of total assimilation, from which they were "saved," ironically, by Egyptian "anti-semitism." A sweet beginning can blind us to deeper consequences. We recall the misleading sweetness of belonging to the majority Egyptian culture which preceded Israel's physical enslavement by our former hosts.

"No Supper Tonight!"

This custom is based on Maimonides. The leaders of the seder begin to remove from the table the plates set in front of the children. When the children ask why, they explain that they are not going to eat until midnight. When the angry protests subside, the leaders can explain that it was all in fun and return the plates. At the same time ask everyone to describe their feelings at the moment the plates were removed. This is exactly what a slave feels – a sense of helplessness and dependency, without rights, a vulnerability in which basic things can be snatched away at any moment for no reason.

"Because I say so!"

The leaders of the seder order a child to perform a task which has no practical purpose – for example dragging out a heavy winter coat and then immediately returning it. When the child protests, the leader can explain that this is a classic example of "harsh labor" ("*be-farech*") to which the Jews in Egypt were subjected. As defined by Jewish law "harsh labor is a task which has no set end or a task which serves no need" (MAIM. LAWS OF SLAVES 1:6). Arbitrary, pointless assignments can seem harsher and more humiliating than useful tasks demanding physical exertion.

A Game Show: "Jeopardy"

The leaders of the seder give answers – and the children have to guess the questions. For example, "open the door," or "maror in charoset," or "blood and the plague of the first-born."

Remember: The Rabbinic principle of education was built on anomaly and spontaneity. You will have to think up new activities every year! For freshness try to ask a participant not leading the seder to think up, in advance, an appropriate surprise, and then spring it on the guests.

In the Vernacular: *Ma Nishtana* in Multiple Languages

The seder is meant to be an inclusive educational experience. For that reason the four questions were often recited not only in Hebrew – but in the native languages of the many lands in which Jews have resided.

With the help of the participants of the seder, you may wish to read the questions in as many languages as possible.

Amharic (Ethiopia)

ይህን ለሊት /ከሌሎች/ለሉቶች ሁሉ በምን ተለየ?
በሌሎች ለሊቶች ሁሉ አንዴ ጊዜስ እንኳን አንነከርም/ማርር/
በዚህ ለሊት ግን ሁለት ጊዜ /እንነክራለን/::

በሌሎች ሁሉ ያልቦካ ወይም የቦካ ቂጣ እንበላለን:: በዚህ
ለሊት ግን ሁሉ ያልቦካ ቂጣ ብቻ::

በሌሎች ሁሉ ሌሎች ቀጠላ ቀጠሎችን ሁሉ እንበላለን፣ በዚህ ጊዜ
ግን መራራ ብቻ::

በሌሎች ሁሉ ተቀምጠን ወይም ዘንበል ብለን እንበላላን፣
እንጠጣለንም:: በዚህ ለሊት ግን ሁላችን ዘንበል ብለን ነው::

Italian

Che differenza c'è fra questa e tutte le altre notti?

Perchè tutte le altre notti possiamo mangiare pane lievitato e azzimo, e questa notte soltanto azzimo; tutte le altre notti possiamo mangiare ogni tipo di verdura, e questa notte l'erba amara; tutte le altre notti non possiamo intingere nemmeno una volta, e questa notte dobbiamo intingere due volte; tutte le altre notti noi mangiamo e beviamo o seduti o appoggiati col gomito, e questa notte siamo tutti appoggiati col gomito?

6

Russian

Чем отличается эта ночь от всех остальных ночей?

Ибо во все ночи едим мы квашеное и опресноки, а в эту ночь – только опресноки.

Ибо во все ночи едим мы разную зелень, а в эту ночь – лишь горькую.

Ибо во все ночи мы ни разу не окунаем (нашу еду), а в эту ночь – дважды.

Ибо во все ночи мы едим либо сидя, либо возлежа, а в эту ночь – все возлежим.

French

Pourquoi cette nuit se distingue-t-elle de toutes les autres nuits? Toutes les autres nuits, nous ne trempons pas (les aliments) même une seule fois et cette nuit nous les trempons deux fois!

Toutes les autres nuits, il nous est permis de manger du pain levé comme du pain azyme, cette nuit seulement du pain azyme!

Toutes les autres nuits nous mangeons des herbes quelconques, cette nuit des herbes amères!

Toutes les autres nuits, nous mangeons et buvons assis ou accoudés, cette nuit nous sommes tous accoudés!

Ladino

Kuanto fue de-mud'ad'a la noçe la esta, mas ke tod'as las noçes.

Ke en tod'as las noçes, non nos entinientes afilu ves una, i la noçe la esta dos vezes.

Ke en tod'as las noçes, nos komientes levdo o sesenia,i la noçe la esta tod'o el sesenia.

Ke en tod'as las noçes nos komientes resto de ved'r'uras, i la noçe la esta liçuga.

Ke en tod'as las noçes, nos komientes i bevientes, tanto asentad'os i tanto areskovdad'os, i la noçe la esta tod'os nos areskovdad'os.

Yiddish

Tate, Ich vil dir fregen di fier kashes:

Vee azoi iz di nacht fun Pesach anders fun alle necht fun a gantz yor?

1. [In] alle necht fun a gantz yor, esn mir chometz un matzo. Ober di nacht fun Pesach, esn mir nor matzo.

2. [In] alle necht fun a gantz yor, esn mir alerley grinsn. Ober di nacht fun Pesach, esn mir nor bitere grinsn.

3. [In] alle necht fun a gantz yor, tunken mir nit ayn, afilyn eyn mol nit. Ober di nacht fun Pesach, tunken mir ayn, tsvey mol — eyn mol chreyn in charoyses, un dos tsveyte mol a tsibele in salts-vaser.

4. [In] alle necht fun a gantz yor, esn mir say zitsindik un say ongelent. Ober di nacht fun Pesach, esn mir ale ongelent.

Dutch

Wat is het verschil tussen deze avond en alle andere avonden?

Op alle andere avonden mogen wij zowel gezuurd als ongezuurd brood eten, op deze avond eten we alleen maar ongezuurd brood.

Want op alle andere avonden mogen wij allerlei soorten groenten eten, op deze avond alleen bitterkruid.

Want op alle andere avonden dopen we ons eten zelfs niet een keer in , op deze avond doen we het zelfs twee maal.

Want op alle andere avonden eten we terwijl we zitten of leunen, op deze avond leunen we de hele tijd.

Spanish

Por qué es diferente esta noche de las demás noches? En todas las noches comemos jametz o matzá, por qué esta noche solamente matzá?

Todas las noches comemos cualquier verdura, por qué esta noche comemos solamente hierbas amargas?

En todas las noches no nos ocurre mojarlas ni une sola vez, por qué esta noche dos veces?

Todas las noches comemos sentados o recostados, por qué esta noche todos comemos recostados?

German

Was macht diese Nacht anders als alle anderen Nächte? An allen andere Nächten essen wir Gesäuertes und Ungesäuertes. Heute Nacht nur Ungesäuertes.

An allen andere Nächten essen wir beliebige Kräuter, in dieser Nacht nur Bitterkraut.

An allen anderen Nächten tunken wir nicht ein, auch nicht ein einziges Mal, heute Nacht zweimal.

An allen anderen Nächten essen wir freisitzend oder angelehnt, heute Nacht nur angelehnt.

Interrogating a Famous Text: Questions and Answers About *Ma Nishtana*

The famous four questions are so well-known, usually recited by heart, that we take them for granted. Upon a second glance, their formulation, their number, their place in the seder and the identity of the speaker are all open to question. Compare these two versions:

Haggadah's Four Questions	*Mishna's Original Three Questions* *
How is this night different from all other nights?	They pour the leader of the seder a second cup of wine and here the son asks. If the child lacks intelligence (*daat*), his father teaches him:
On all other nights, we eat either leavened bread or matza, but on this night we eat only matza.	Look, how different this night is from all other nights!
On all other nights, we eat other kinds of vegetables, but on this night we eat maror (bitter herbs).	On all other nights, we dip once, this night twice.
On all other nights, we need not dip our vegetables even once, but on this night we do so twice.	On all other nights, we eat leavened bread and matza, this night, only matza.
On all other nights, we eat either sitting upright or reclining, but on this night we all recline.	On all other nights, we eat meat roasted, fried or cooked, this night only roasted.
	According to the intelligence of the child the father teaches him.

* (PESACHIM 10:4 ACCORDING TO THE PARMA MANUSCRIPT, ONE OF THE MOST RELIABLE ANCIENT MANUSCRIPTS)

Questions:

#1 — Numbering, A Matter of Punctuation

How many questions are there really? Where do we insert question marks and periods? Is there perhaps only one question: *"How is this night different?"* and four answers describing the rituals? Perhaps there are four aspects of the same question: *"Why is this night different in that . . . ?"*

#2 — Who Asks Whom?

In the Mishna the four "questions" are attributed to the parent who teaches the son: *"Look how different this night is . . . ."* But everyone knows the custom that the youngest child is supposed to recite them. What is the origin of the contradiction between the Mishna and our customs today? Who is supposed to ask whom?

#3 — Timing

Isn't this the wrong time in the seder for a child to ask these questions? How can one ask *"why do we eat maror"* and *"why do we dip twice,"* if at this point in the seder we have only eaten celery dipped once in salt water?

#4 — Disappearing Questions

The Mishna version records only *three* questions! Questions about *maror* and reclining are missing. Instead a question about roasted meat appears. Why these changes?

Answers:

#1 — How Many Questions Are There?

The famous "four questions" ("vier kashas" in Yiddish) are never called by that name in the sources. Perhaps the original intent of these so called "questions" is radically different than the usual practice. It all depends on how we translate the Hebrew interrogative *"ma:"* "how," or "why," or "look, how."

If "*ma*" means "**how** is this night different?," then we have *one* question with four answers describing ritual behaviors. The child who asks the question in this light is concerned with following the extraordinary etiquette of this evening banquet. The parent must guide the child to participate appropriately, to do the mitzvot like a grownup.

If "*ma*" means "**why**," then the child is asking *four* questions which all begin alike: *"Why* is this night different than all other nights regarding . . . ." The inquirer seeks reasons, not merely rules. The parent must explain the historical origins and philosophic purposes of each particular custom, though the answers are nowhere to be found in the traditional printed Haggadah.

#2 — Who Asks Whom? Who Is Speaking?

If *"ma"* means "**look, how**!" — an exclamation of surprise accompanied generally by a pointing index finger, then the speaker is probably the parent, not the child. In the Mishna it is the parent who "instructs the child without knowledge" by pointing out: *"Look how different this night is from all other nights."* The four questions become four curious behaviors that ought to arouse wonder, for amazement is the beginning of the search for knowledge. The parent must know how to "open up" the youngest child who doesn't even know how to formulate questions. For example, "Listen dear, let's look around and see what surprises are planned for us during tonight's meal." Hopefully, the child will not only respond with that "Aha" experience of eyes opened wide, but also add his own comments to the parent's four. Under no circumstances should this be merely a ritualized recitation of questions by the parent or the young child.

In fact, the "four questions" are not obligatory at all. As a medieval Spanish rabbi explained: **"It is a mitzvah to tell the story of the exodus from Egypt by arousing one's mind and heart and drawing the things out of us. Everyone should ask their parent or anyone sitting beside them at the table to explain the reason for each and every thing. Even if one is alone at home and knows all the reasons, one should conduct a discussion with oneself, asking and answering one's own questions."**

(*HAGGADAH, MEAM LOEZ, PAGE 234-236, HEBREW EDITION*)

It is now obvious why the traditional numbering of the questions at "four" is merely a convenience for remembering the various parts of the seder: the four cups, the four children and the four questions. However, in fact, the number and content of the questions are as numerous and pliant in form as the curiosity and the imagination of the child.

#3 — Poor Timing

It is manifestly absurd for a young child to ask at this point in the seder about dipping and eating maror. At best, the young

child — so concretely oriented — might inquire about reclining (as the first cup of wine is drunk while reclining on pillows) and about the matza (just broken and the afikoman hidden). To recite all these questions at this inappropriate moment is to formalize a performance betraying its estrangement from its original function. It is better to view the questions as examples of the kind of issues to be pointed out by the parent and raised by all the participants during the seder — as things come up. The "four questions" signal the beginning of an ongoing inquiry that must be initiated here even before the telling of the story.

#4 — Disappearing Questions

At first glance, one notices the *difference* between the traditional four questions and the more ancient version preserved in the Mishna. Here we have a lesson about the historical development of the questions.

In the days of the Temple, and some scholars believe for a short period thereafter, Jews strictly observed the commandment to eat the Pesach lamb broiled over an open fire as required on the night of the exodus from Egypt. *"They shall eat it roasted over the fire, with unleavened bread and bitter herbs."* (EXODUS 12:8) Barbecued meat cooks more quickly, so many commentators explain the concern for roast lamb with the subsequent verse, *"this is how you shall eat it; your loins girded, your sandals on your feet and your staff in your hand; and you shall eat it hurriedly; it is a Passover offering to the Lord."* (EXODUS 12:11)

However, when the Temple was destroyed, sacrifices stopped. Gradually it became accepted not to eat lamb on Pesach, especially not roast lamb because it might seem as if the lamb were a sacrifice and as if sacrifices outside the Temple were permitted.

Clearly, if the question were to remain relevant to the experience of the child, this question about roast meat had to be replaced. The Haggadah substituted the question on the bitter herbs, which were originally part of the Pesach sacrifice, but were continued as an independent practice even without the Pesach lamb.

As we noted, the older and more reliable manuscripts of the Mishna (such as the one from Parma quoted above) record only *three* questions. In the Haggadah a fourth question has been added, perhaps to reflect the theme of organization in "fours" characteristic of other features of the Haggadah. The fourth question is about "reclining." This question seems to have originated in Babylonia which was not part of the Roman Empire or its cultural milieu. Reclining on sofas around small tables at festive meals reflects the practice of the Greco-Roman upper class. It was part of the mandatory practice of the seder night when every Jew was meant to feel part of a free nobility. In Babylonia, where reclining was not the normal practice, this custom on Pesach was unusual and noteworthy, calling forth a question. **Wonder arises spontaneously out of the discrepancy between the everyday and the extraordinary.**

Quotations to Encourage A Questioning Mind

Questioning is often seen as the distinguishing mark of the Jew. Using these quotations you may wish to lead a discussion on the value of asking questions. Ask people to pick their favorite quotation and to explain their choice.

1 *It is an old saying: Ask a Jew a question, and the Jew answers with a question. Every answer given arouses new questions. The progress of knowledge is matched by an increase in the hidden and mysterious.*
— RABBI LEO BAECK, *JUDAISM AND SCIENCE* (GERMANY, 1949)

2 *Whoever is ashamed to ask,*
Will diminish in wisdom among men.
— MOSES IBN EZRA, *SHIRAT YISRAEL* (SPAIN, 11TH C.)

3 *Whoever is not ashamed to ask,*
Will in the end be exalted.
— SAMUEL BEN NAHMAN, *B.T. BERACHOT* 63B (3RD C. BABYLONIA)

4 *If disciples know that their teacher is able to answer them, then they may ask. Otherwise they may not pose the question (and embarrass their teacher).*
— BABYLONIAN TALMUD, *HULLIN* 6

5 *A wise person's question is half the answer.*
— SHLOMO IBN GABIROL (SPAIN, 1050)

6 *The truly wise question the wisdom of others because they question their own wisdom as well, the foolish, because it is different from their own.*
— RABBI LEOPOLD STEIN, *JOURNEY INTO THE SELF* (GERMANY, 1810-1882)

7 *What is a human being after all but a question? One is here to ask and only to ask, to ask honestly and boldly, and to wait humbly for an answer.*
— RACHEL VARNHAGEN (GERMAN SALON LEADER, 1771-1833),
LETTER TO ADAM VON MULLER, DEC. 15, 1820

8 *Be swift to hear, but with patience make reply.*
— BEN SIRA, 5.11 (ISRAEL, 2ND C. B.C.E.)

9 *Our little children know how to ask good questions. We evade answering them.*
— ISRAEL ELDAD, "THE VICTORY OF THE WISE SON," *HEGYONOT CHAZAL*

10 *Unless you call out, who will answer the door?*
— ETHIOPIAN PROVERB

11 *Hillel would say: the bashful pupil cannot learn and the pedantic (overly strict, quick-to-anger) teacher cannot teach.*
— *PIRKEI AVOT* 3:5 (1ST C. C.E.)

12 *A theology student once asked Martin Luther, "What did God do before He created the world?" And his answer was, "God was making hell, for those who are inquisitive."*
— MARTIN LUTHER (GERMANY, 16TH C.)

6

Chapter 7
Storytelling — Maggid

Role-Playing at the Seder:
Experiencing the Exodus

■ *by Aliza Arzt* (adapted by Noam Zion)

*"In every generation all are obligated to see themselves as
  if they went out of Egypt"*
                                              — *The Haggadah.*

The goal of the seder is to reexperience personally the pain of slavery and the exhilaration of liberation. Role-playing is a wonderful tool to achieve this goal. Without any specialized dramatic skills and with little knowledge it is still easy to involve the participants in a simple role-play. A role-play — unlike a play — involves no costumes or set script. One needs to improvise orally while sitting in one's seat at the table. A prop can be made at home to concretize the role being performed.

The following pages should be mailed to each participant in the seder well before the seder itself. Children as young as six should be included. Everyone should be given ample time to prepare before the seder. It is best to consult with the leader on the choice of parts. (This activity may replace the Rabbinic midrash *"Arami Oved Avi"* in the Haggadah — see page 78.)

Directions for Preparations:

1. Choose a **category** based upon who you are (child, adolescent, Jewish man or woman, senior, non-Jew, Jewish leader).

2. Read the description of who you are and what your life is like during the time when you are a slave in Egypt. (The printed descriptions are merely suggestive. Feel free to use your imagina-

Aliza Arzt is a member of Havurat Shalom, Boston.

tion. If you wish, read Exodus 1-2; 5-14, or other resource books.)

3. Choose one of the following **scenes:** A. *Living as a Slave*, or B. *Leaving Egypt*; and answer the questions for that scene (you don't have to write down the answers, just know what you would say to answer them).

4. Choose at least one of the **project** ideas and bring the completed project to the seder to use as a prop in the role-play:
   • *Make a banner that you would carry leaving Egypt.*
   • *Write a letter to an Egyptian friend your age, one you had made while you were a slave.*
   • *Draw a picture of one of your experiences during this story.*
   • *Make a scroll that you would bury in Egypt or at the Red Sea with some kind of record (writing or drawing) of what happened to you, for someone to find in the future.*
   • *Make a simple mask expressing your feelings (sad, happy, angry, scared) about a particular event in the story.*
   • *Bring an object that might have been a memento from Egypt.*

At the Seder:

The "narrator" will tell the story, scene by scene. At the beginning of each scene, the narrator will ask those in this scene to introduce themselves: "Who are you?" The person then reads or summarizes the description of who he or she is.

Next, the narrator will ask you to tell "What happened?" Answer according to the questions you prepared.

Finally, the narrator will ask: "What have you brought to show us?" You show everyone your project and explain what it is.

The Narrator's Part

The narrator must read all the roles in advance and review the questions to be asked. The narrator must be able to read slowly and clearly and to improvise as the interviews are conducted. (Don't let anyone go on too long.)

Scene A: Living as a Slave in Egypt

Jacob went down to Egypt with 70 descendants. As the years passed, we, his children, grew to be a great multitude and the Egyptians, fearing us, enslaved us. Pharaoh and the taskmasters worked us hard, and when this did not diminish us, he commanded that every baby boy be thrown in the Nile.

Who would like to be interviewed about their slavery time in Egypt? *(People who prepared for this section.)*

Who are you? *(a Jewish man, child, etc.)*

What happened to you? *(Probe according to the role of each character, encouraging improvisation based on Scene "A" — see pages 42-43.)*

What have you brought to remind us of your time in Egypt? *(They answer by showing and telling about their "project.")*

Scene B: Leaving Egypt

Moses and Aaron were sent to rescue our people. At first, even we did not listen to them because we were so weary from our labors. Then they brought wondrous things — 10 plagues. Before the 10th plague, we were commanded to kill, roast and eat a lamb and smear the blood on our doorposts. We were set free, but the Egyptians would not let us go unharmed and they came after us with soldiers and chariots. God provided yet another miracle and the Red (Reed) Sea split open for us.

Who would like to be interviewed about the Exodus? *(People who prepared for this section.)*

Who are you? *(a Jewish man, child, etc.)*

What happened to you? *(Ask the questions for the appropriate role for scene "B" — see pages 42-43.)*

What have you brought to remind us of your Exodus from Egypt? *(They answer by showing and telling about their "Project.")*

Conclusion:

And now, as we recall these events and as we try to place ourselves into the minds and hearts of those who experienced them, we thank God that we can sit here tonight, in freedom, to retell the story. We hope that we will be able to show empathy with those who experience a similar fate.

Scene C: Singing our Redemption

All sing together:

"LET MY PEOPLE GO"

An Afro-American Spiritual

When Israel was in Egypt's land:
"Let My people go" (EXODUS 5:1).
Oppressed so hard they could not stand,
"Let My people go."

*Go down, Moses, way down in Egypt's land,
Tell old Pharaoh: "Let My people go."*

Thus said the Lord, bold Moses said,
"Let My people go."
If not, I'll smite your first-born dead,
"Let My people go."

*Go down, Moses, way down in Egypt's land,
Tell old Pharaoh: "Let My people go."*

No more shall they in bondage toil,
"Let My people go. "
If they come out with Egypt's spoil,
"Let My people go."

*Go down, Moses, way down in Egypt's land,
Tell old Pharaoh: "Let my people go."*

SEE NEXT PAGES FOR PARTICIPANT PARTS

THE PARTICIPANTS' PARTS

I. CATEGORY: CHILD

Description: You are one of the children who are slaves. The children worked in the fields with their parents 6 days a week. They only had to work 8 hours a day instead of 12 hours. The children had these jobs: helping their parents with their jobs (gathering straw, bringing food and water to everyone, preparing the food, making bricks, and taking care of the youngest children (up to age 3, usually their brothers, sisters and cousins). When the children were not working, they sometimes had school taught by the older people, even though the Egyptians didn't like to see them studying. They would learn how to read and write and learn the stories of their people. There was very little time to play. If the children were seen playing, someone would probably find a job for them to do.

Tasks: Please prepare yourself to play in one of these two scenes and to do a project.

Scene A: Living as a Slave (type of work, task masters, throwing the boys into the Nile, Moses' killing of the taskmaster, etc).

Tasks:

1. Describe what you would do during a typical day.
2. What would you do on Shabbat when you didn't have to work for the Egyptians?
3. What do you think things will be like when you grow up?
4. What things do you like most and hate most about your life now?

or

Scene B : Leaving Egypt (the plagues, killing the lamb and the blood on the doorpost, the matza, crossing the Red Sea)

1. What was the scariest thing that happened to you during the Exodus?
2. What did you take as a souvenir from Egypt?
3. What did you think of Moses and Aaron and Miriam? Did you ever get to see them? When?
4. Did anything happen that you didn't understand? What was it?
5. What was it like crossing the Red Sea?
6. How do you feel about what happened to the Egyptians? About God's role in your escape?

Project: Making props. (*See the directions on page 30, #4*)

II. CATEGORY: ADOLESCENT

Description: You are about to become 13, the age when people begin to make the transition from childhood to adulthood. Your parents have probably been working to make this change more gradual for you, by gradually increasing their expectations even though you technically don't have to work a full day, or do the adult jobs. However, when you reach 13, it will be the Egyptian taskmasters making sure you do your 12 hours of work, not just your parents. You may be assigned a job away from the people you have come to know. You will be required to report to a taskmaster for your instructions. You have managed to learn to read and write and enjoy these activities very much, but you know that in a few weeks, you will not have time to do this anymore. You are unsure of how you will fit in to your new role, and before you have much of a chance to find out, the plagues and the Exodus begin and you are catapulted into a new life.

Tasks:

Please choose one scene and prepare for your role with the help of the following questions and do a project.

Scene A: Living as a Slave (type of work, taskmasters, throwing baby boys in the Nile, Moses kills the taskmaster)

1. How have you been prepared to take on the work of an adult?
2. What are you most anxious about and most excited about in becoming an adult?
3. What do you think things will be like during the next 5 years?
4. What things do you like most and hate most about your life now?

or

Scene B : Leaving Egypt (the plagues, killing the lamb and the blood on the doorpost, the matza, crossing the Red Sea)

1. Describe your feelings about these events. Were they different from what you had expected would happen? Give examples if possible.
2. What did you take from Egypt?
3. What did you think of Moses and Aaron and Miriam? Did you even get to see them? When?
4. Did anything happen that you didn't understand? What was it?
5. What was it like crossing the Reed Sea?
6. How do you feel about what happened to the Egyptians? About God's Role in the Exodus?

Project: Making props. (*See the directions on page 30, #4*)

III. CATEGORY: JEWISH MAN

Description: Slavery and work are all you've ever known and all you've seen your parents and grandparents do. When you were a child, you learned about your people's history through songs and stories, but you have not had much time to think about that since you became a man. You work 12 hours a day for the Egyptians making bricks, preparing food, building, excavating, gathering supplies. You never know what work you will be given or where you will be asked to work. Frequently, the work you are asked to do is demeaning: work you consider to be for women, or work beyond your strength. When work is done, you must work more hours in your home to take care of your few possessions and to tend your animals. If you are married, you have little time for your wife. You know what will happen if she should bear a son, so you have considered (or are already) sleeping apart from her so she will not conceive a child. Sometimes you feel that the only way out of slavery is to refuse to bring another generation into such a world.

Tasks: Prepare to role-play one of these scenes and to do one project:

Scene A: Living as a Slave (type of work, taskmasters, Pharaoh's daughter saves Moses, later Moses kills a taskmaster).

1. Do you ever reflect on your life, and if so, what are your thoughts?
2. What would you do if you were able to do whatever you wanted to the Egyptians?
3. What are your fantasies about the kind of life you would like to lead?
4. What are the biggest drawbacks and biggest benefits about your life as it is?
5. What does "being Hebrew" mean to you? What role models do you have for your children?
6. Do you think it is easier for a man to withstand oppression as compared to a woman?

or

Scene B : Leaving Egypt (the plagues, killing the lamb, "borrowing" things from the Egyptians, crossing the Red Sea)

1. What was your reaction to the plagues?
2. What have you learned about God from the things you witnessed?
3. What do you expect will be different in your life now that you have left Egypt?
4. What did you do when you were told to step into the Red Sea? What did this teach you about yourself?

Project: Making props. (*See the directions on page 30, #4*)

IV. CATEGORY: JEWISH WOMAN

Description: Slavery and work are all you've ever known and all you've seen for your parents and grandparents. When you were a child, you learned about your people's history though songs and stories, but you have not had much time to think about that since you became a woman. You work 12 hours a day for the Egyptians making bricks, preparing food, building, excavating, gathering supplies. You never know what work you will be given or where you will be asked to work. Frequently the work you are asked to do is demeaning: men's work beyond your strength, work with people much older or younger, work with men who look at you in a way that makes you uncomfortable and who make suggestive remarks to you. You know you must always guard your virtue but you are frightened when you are alone in the city that is being built. When work is done, you must work more hours in your home to prepare food, make, clean and mend clothes, keep the house clean. If you are married, you have little time for your husband. You know what will happen if you should bear a son, so you try not to entice your husband, but you wish he would want to be with you more often. Maybe he is worried about the same things you are. Sometimes you feel that the only way out of slavery is to refuse to bring another generation into such a world.

Tasks: Prepare yourself to play one of these scenes and to do a small project.

Scene A: Living as a Slave (type work, attitude to ethnic strangers, to slave women, taskmasters, Pharaoh's daughter saves baby boy thrown into the Nile, Moses kills the taskmaster).

1. Do you ever reflect on your life, and if so, what are your thoughts?
2. What would you do if you were able to do whatever you wanted to the Egyptians? What would you do to protect your children?
3. What are your fantasies about the kind of life you would like to lead?
4. What are the biggest drawbacks and biggest benefits about your life as it is?
5. What does "being a Hebrew woman" mean to you?
6. Do you think it is easier for a woman to cope with slavery?

or

Scene B : Leaving Egypt (the plagues, killing the lamb, "borrowing" things from the Egyptians, crossing the Reed Sea)

1. What was your reaction to the plagues?
2. What have you learned about God from the things you witnessed?
3. Have your feelings about what God has done affected your idea of what it means to be a "woman?" How?
4. What do you expect will be different in your life now that you have left Egypt?
5. What did you do when you were told to step into the Red Sea? What did this teach you about yourself?
6. What will you tell your children about Egypt or the Exodus?

Project: Prepare props for the role-play. *(See the directions on page 41, #4)*

V. CATEGORY: ELDERLY

Description: You live the life of a man or woman slave. You are aging and feel the effects of the hard labor more every year. There is no respite for the older worker in the eyes of the Egyptians, although sometimes the young adults are able to help you. You see that joy and wonder have been extinguished from the eyes of your children as they come to resemble you more and more. You may be a grandparent, or are thinking about what that may be like. This brings up memories of your own childhood, young adulthood and your parents and grandparents. You have heard Moses' demands and God's promises, but you are unsure whether you want to join the movement to leave Egypt.

Tasks: Prepare a role-play for one of these scenes, and a small project:

Scene A: Living as a Slave

1. Do you ever reflect on your life, and if so, what are your thoughts?
2. Do you feel you are still able to protect or aid your children? How?
3. How do you feel about what your children are like as adults?
4. What advice would you give your children as they grow older and become parents themselves?
5. Do you feel that you have attained any wisdom? Explain.
6. What does "being an Israelite" mean to you?

or

Scene B : Leaving Egypt (the plagues, killing the lamb, "borrowing" things from the Egyptians, crossing the Red Sea)

1. What was your reaction to the plagues, especially the tenth plague?
2. What have you learned about God from the things you witnessed?
3. How has your experience leaving Egypt affected your assumptions about what your life will be like? How has it affected your children?
4. What did you do when you were told to step into the Red Sea? What did this teach you about yourself?

Project: Making props for the role-play. *(See the directions on page 41, #4)*

VI. CATEGORY: EGYPTIAN

Description: You are, by birth, an Egyptian or a member of a group which is neither Israelite nor Egyptian. You feared the population growth of the Hebrews, but opposed the throwing of the baby boys into the Nile. You benefited from slavery. Now you have experienced the plagues that the God of Israel brought and it has frightened or greatly affected you. You no longer feel safe in your own land.

Tasks: Prepare yourself to play one of these scenes and to do one project.

Scene A: Living in the era when the Hebrews are slaves

1. Do you ever reflect on your life, and if so, what are your thoughts?
2. What are the biggest drawbacks and biggest benefits about your life as it is?
3. How did you feel about Pharaoh's plan? About the midwives? About Pharaoh's daughter's adoption of Moses?
4. What was your first response to Moses' demand?

or

Scene B: Living during the Exodus and the splitting of the Red Sea

1. What was your reaction to the plagues?
2. What have you learned about Israel's God from the things you witnessed?
3. What did you do when you were told to follow Israel into the Red Sea? What did this teach you about yourself?
4. What do you think will occur in Egyptian society after the traumatic Exodus of Israel?

Project: Making props for the role-play. *(See the directions on page 41, #4)*

VII. CATEGORY: THE JEWISH LEADER: MOSES, AARON, or MIRIAM

Description: You grew up with an exceptionally strong mother who hid her baby from Pharaoh and then agreed to his adoption by Pharaoh's daughter to save his life. Later you took part in the "Let My People Go" movement whether through physical violence (killing the Egyptian taskmaster), through negotiations or through wonders. You must mediate between a demanding God and a hesitant enslaved people. You must collaborate with your siblings in a tense situation where the youngest is God's chosen leader.

Tasks: Prepare to role-play one of the scenes and prepare a project for the scene.

Scene A: Confronting a Slave People

1. What bothered you most about the way the slaves responded to the taskmasters?
2. Describe your mother's special strength. What nourished it? Was your father as strong as she was? What have you tried to learn from her model?
3. How did you feel when you first heard God's promises to redeem the people and your appointed mission within the Divine plan?

or

Scene B: Leaving Egypt

1. What difficulties did you have with your siblings and their roles in the "Let My People Go" movement?
2. How did the people and Pharaoh respond to you as the bearer of God's message? What doubts of your own did you feel?
3. What lessons did you learn from negotiating with Pharaoh?
4. How did you feel about the role of violence in the liberation (plagues, Red Sea, etc.) ?

Project: Making props for the role-play. *(See the directions on page 41, #4)*

7

Bibliodrama:
Theory and Practice for Beginners

■ *by Peter Pitzele* (adapted by Noam Zion)

Introduction

Peter Pitzele*, a master of improvised role playing on Biblical themes, lays out the rudiments of his approach. The leader of the seder or a participant with drama or family therapy background can readily utilize the tools described below to personalize the Exodus in surprising ways. The interpretation of the Biblical story in drama is an analogue to the Rabbinic midrash that is at the center of the Haggadah.

Bibliodrama and Midrash

Bibliodrama is a form of improvisational role-playing in which the roles played are taken from Biblical texts. The roles may be those of characters who appear in the Bible or parts may be further expanded to include certain objects or images in the Bible which may be embodied in voice and action (the serpent in the garden or the staff of Moses). I call my work **Bibliodrama**, with a capital B. (By capitalizing the word I meant Bibliodrama to refer explicitly to the Bible as the source for dramatic exploration).

Bibliodrama is a creative and expressive mode of Biblical interpretation; it is a form of midrashic play. Midrash is an immensely long tradition of commentary, storytelling, and imaginative interpretation of the Bible which sought to fill in the gaps in narrative, address textual contradictions and inconsistencies, and weave in applications to contemporary life. Though at times a deeply scholarly enterprise, there is also something folkloric about midrash. It belongs to an oral tradition, holy and still evolving, which continues to respond to the Bible in fresh ways. The country of midrash is vast, anonymous, democratic, and inexhaustible. Profound readers with glittering eyes have been there before me: many of their achievements are in the record books of Rabbinic Midrash, but the field of play welcomes new players. Each generation can go

*Dr. Peter Pitzele, author of Digging Our Fathers' Wells: A Personal Encounter with the Myths of Genesis, *combined a literature and psychotherapy background to create a center for Bibliodrama. This selection comes from his forthcoming* Scripture Windows.

there for fresh discoveries. My Bibliodrama seeks to join this conversation with the Bible that has been going on for thousands of years.

The Midrashic Space

Bibliodrama begins with acts of reading. One reads the words on the page, and one reads into the spaces between the words on the page. There is a traditional commentary that talks about the Bible as having been written in black letters and white letters. The black letters are those that form the words; the white letters are those made up of the negative spaces the black letters create. The black letters are fixed for all time; the white letters are perpetually new. Bibliodrama is a game played in the open spaces of the text for which the black letters are the boundaries.

To role play with creativity and depth one must develop a midrashic imagination; one must get a sense of how great interpretive imaginations find and fill the white spaces. **The purpose of this training is not only to learn from the masters, it is to liberate your own imagination, to give yourself permission to embroider and to embellish the text, to invent new midrash and to inspire others to do the same.**

Midrash permitted me my own creative response to the biblical narrative. One did not need to be a learned scholar or a sophisticated literary critic. Midrash had the quality of folklore. Midrash was really a way of asking and answering questions, and even a child could do that, sometimes more piercingly than adults. For all the time I had put in as a sometime professor of literature, I had never been invited to create with the creator. I could tell you a lot about Hamlet, but no one ever suggested that a legitimate form of Shakespearean commentary might be to write my own soliloquy. Yet here was the Bible, a text more sacred than Shakespeare, and there existed a tradition of interpretation that sanctioned a **participatory creativity**.

What actually occurs when one begins to read midrashically is that one reads very slowly in order to see each verb and predicate as a cinematographer might see them. One becomes aware of the ways one is unconsciously filling in detail the narrative itself does not specify. One learns to imagine various different ways that filling in might be done. And one learns then to ask questions about these negative spaces, so that one can become aware of the interpretive possibilities they provide.

[*Editor:* For example in Exodus 2:5-6 we read that Pharaoh's daughter opens the little ark (basket) with the infant Moses, she sees the child crying, feels empathy and says: "This is one of the Hebrew children." Reading slowly we identify interpretive gaps: Did Pharaoh's daughter get down on her knees to see the baby? Did she open the basket slowly and suspiciously or excitedly like a little girl receiving a surprise gift? What passed through her mind as she acknowledged this baby to be one of the Hebrews her father had ordered drowned?]

Bibliodrama: The Tools

The essence of Bibliodrama is the act of voicing and playing a biblical character. One can do this singly or in a group with others. No props or devices are needed to accomplish this. When the warm-up is sound, the invitation made safe and appealing, the scene and characters clearly defined, then the act of voicing and playing is as easy as a somersault.

However, for the would-be director there are a number of tools that can support and extend this bibliodramatic move. Casting a scene and interviewing the characters is first. Another tool involves the use of **empty chairs** to block a scene, or to symbolize an internal state. Another is **echoing**, the use of your voice in a kind of elaboration of what the players say that helps them sustain and deepen their role playing.

A fourth tool is **doubling**, which refers to the method by which more than one person can develop a biblical character in a kind of midrashic tag-team match. A fifth technique involves animating objects, turning Moses' staff, for example, into a **talking object**. Finally there is **dramatic dialogue**, the encounter of powerful biblical characters who are encouraged to speak to one another openly, even though in the story they may not have been able to express themselves frankly.

1. Casting a Scene and Interviewing the Characters

[*Editor:* You might introduce a bibliodramatic exercise in the following way: I have always been intrigued by Exodus 5, Moses' first encounter with Pharaoh after receiving his commission at the burning bush. Let's read it slowly and then I'd like to invite you to do something a little different. Let's make a list of all the possible characters who might appear — even if unnamed — in this episode (Moses, Aaron, Pharaoh, the Egyptian advisors, Miriam, Pharaoh's daughter, the Jewish leaders or an Egyptian priest).]

Let's create some midrash together. I want you to select one of these characters and for a moment to become that character. I'd like to get your perspective on what happened today. Raise your hand when you know who you are. You can pass if you don't feel like doing midrash in this way. Hands go up. Not all. Not all need to play, and I need to make sure people feel free to watch. People warm-up differently to this kind of work; there are always fast-starters, usually enough to get things moving. But it's a good idea as well as good teaching to check in at various points to see if any of the people who were quiet at the beginning would like to ask a question if not take a part as things are moving along. The ability to include the less willing, if only as interested auditors who with you are learning all sorts of things, comes with practice.

I play the **role of the interviewer**, asking questions as if I had a microphone in my hand. Though I know the story, I pretend to a certain naiveté. That naiveté keeps me fresh and open to the surprising things I might hear. The better I can imagine myself there in the scene, the more lively and curious I become as interviewer. I may have heard certain rumors for which I am trying to get confirmation. Questions, questions, questions: these are the means by which the bibliodramatic facilitator gets people involved in the play.

Using this simple technique, both the group and the facilitator have a chance to experience this form of midrash-making. These 'short-takes' are to Bibliodrama what snorkeling is to scuba diving. Many lovers of the coral never strap on tanks to dive the outer reefs. In time and with a growing confidence and curiosity, the careful swimmer may attempt those challenges. But there is always plenty to see close to shore. The drama moves forward increment by increment by means of the questions asked. Questions, like prompts, send the participant off in certain directions (emotion? information? thoughts? playful invention? external detail? relationship?).

2. Using Empty Chairs

It is best to take the process in stages. In the first stage people are asked to think of a biblical character in the Exodus (like Pharaoh, the midwives, Moses, Aaron, Miriam, Pharaoh's daughter) that interests them, or one that pops into mind and seems to intrigue them. Then in the second stage, people are asked to introduce themselves to the group as that character. You might say something like this: "Having selected a character that interests you, now step into the shoes of that character, and introduce yourself to us. If you don't feel like trying this out, just say 'I pass' when your turn comes."

[*Editor:* For example, in Exodus 5, Moses and his brother Aaron confront Pharaoh in God's name. Pharaoh then pressures the Hebrews who then blame Moses who in turn blames God.]

You can place an **empty chair** in the center of the room and tell the players that this chair represents God, and that they are to stand as near or as far from that chair as they feel represents their closeness or distance from God. Characters may then be questioned about their feelings, relationship, history with God). Once these tableaux are created, the facilitator's task is to interview the participants in role and to help them tell the group a little about themselves. Often other characters will take part in asking characters questions.

Often it will be helpful to ask people once they have chosen the character and become it, to locate that character in time and space. "You tell me you are Miriam? So at what point in your story are you coming before us?" Sometimes the participant may answer immediately and with certainty. "I am Miriam; I have just seen my brother's wife Zipporah." Other times when the character draws a blank you may need to present some of the options: "Are you Miriam as a young girl, as the leader crossing the Red Sea, as the dancer, as the prophetess, as the woman who challenges her brother, as the stricken Miriam, as Miriam dying?"

Note: Focussing the player in on the part, on the particulars, deepens the imaginative connection. Deepening in Bibliodrama always involves tapping into the players' unconscious, for the imagination is a function of our spontaneity, and spontaneity draws its energy from the unreflective, prompt expression of our unconscious minds. Work with characters of the sort I am describing here has its deep-water perils for the novice facilitator; often the unconscious connection, the reasons why one person chooses a certain character, can open up deep places in our souls. It is best when doing this kind of work not to question or probe too far. Help the player to tell a little story in role. Even though you may sense that more could be told, even though you sense the unexpressed feelings (anguish, anger, fear, loss), let the story stand as presented. It will be enough. It will demonstrate the vitality and richness of this method; it will give you a sense of the possibilities of this form of study; it will create

some brilliant midrash. Bibliodrama can be fully alive without necessarily getting "deep."

As the director, you face the group. Let's sat that as part of your warm-up with them, you want to explain what midrash is. You set out two empty chairs, placing one behind the other. "The first chair," you explain, "represents the words on the page. We can all see them; we all agree on what they are. This second chair," now pointing to the chair concealed behind the first, "is all these words can mean and allude to, all the things that these words open up and invite us to imagine or speculate about. This second chair is midrash."

Or as the director you want to develop two opposing sides of a single biblical character. [*Editor:* Let's say the group is exploring Moses' ambivalence about the killing of the Egyptian. The Bible says Moses "looked this way and that way" as he hesitated before the fateful act. Put two chairs back to back representing Moses' weighing the decision to act or not to act. Ask the group to offer thoughts and feelings for each opposing side. You may want a vocal interpreter to sit in one of Moses' chairs and continue the role play.]

The empty chair serves both to concretize a dimension of the character and provide a staging point for its expression. Using the chair also cleanly demarcates the playing space from the group space, the stage from the audience. To reach the chair one moves from audience to participant, from self to role; and then returning to one's seat, one steps out of the role and back into the place of observation.

Empty chairs may be used to sculpt a scene before one actually has people play the parts. You may place chairs side by side, or three chairs together with one off alone — you and the group may play with the relationships between the characters. Once the chairs are arranged, their positions — opposition, alliance, isolation — help the players warm up to the parts. The chairs give some form and control to the interpretive direction of a scene. The chairs support the players and move them in a certain direction. Rearrange the chairs, and new bibliodramatic interpretations present themselves.

3. Doubling

As the director, I am concerned to diversify our sense of Moses. How many Moshes can we get dancing on the pinhead of this verse? I do not move the Bibliodrama either in the direction of various interactions among characters nor of the development of a single coherent characterization. When the goal is to compound versions of the same character at the same moment, doubling becomes the method. Doubling allows you to hatch multiple dramatic possibilities from a single dramatic moment.

Its great virtue is in allowing observers to become participants in the action if only for a single line. Observers may leap in with a phrase or a brief soliloquy and step out again without feeling stage-fright or the burden of having to stand in for a fuller development of their characterization. Doubling serves to keep the Bibliodrama open to fresh insight and to the movement of group members from the periphery to the center.

As the director I prepare the moment for group doubling in the following way: "What I'd like to do at this point is see how many different possible Moshes we might be able to give voice to in this moment of his exile. In Bibliodrama this is called doubling and it can amount to a piling up or a piling on of interpretations which can be quite inconsistent with one another. "So," I continue, "Moshe, what is this moment like for you, this moment when you are standing at the burning bush (Exodus 3) and confronting God's command and commission to return to your long lost family and to confront Pharaoh from whose wrath you fled?"

This wonderful welter of interpretive possibilities is made possible by my invitation to the group to double Moshe. In doing this we suspend the forward momentum of our reading to open up a series of snapshots of Moshe in different moods and poses at this particular moment in his "life."

4. Echoing

Very often in the course of a bibliodramatic exercise, the participants, at least at first, are shy and slow to warm-up. In answer to your questions, their responses are often brief and tentative. Sometimes they fall out of role, and you, as the director, can almost hear the hiss of the energy escaping through the cracks in their partial participation. The technique of echoing can help you to help your players enter more fully into their parts.

Echoing is part of the art of listening. To echo well is to listen well. One listens not just to what is being said, but also what is being implied in a player's voicing of a part. I think of echoing as **creative repetition**. If I were to use empty chairs to demon-

strate echoing I would place two chairs in line, one behind the other. In the first chair are the words I hear from the participant; in the second chair are the feelings and thoughts I imagine might lie behind those words. In echoing I give voice to the participant's second chair. It is my midrash on their midrash. Echoing often makes use of a prompt word or an incomplete sentence which the participant then fills.

Let's say we have been reading the story (Exodus 3:1-10) of the birth and adoption of Moses. Using a variety of **indirect methods**, we may be looking at the social condition of slavery, thinking about repressive regimes, discussing the role women play in the opening chapters of the book, noticing literary motifs, studying the Hebrew, talking about our own experiences of feeling trapped, threatened, exiled. All these are part of the repertoire of methods of Bible study. But then, as the director, I might invite the group to zoom in on Moses' sister, **Miriam**. We might wonder what it was like for her to see a baby brother born in the time of the edict. Such speculation is still indirect (we are talking about her), until a moment comes when I say, *"I wonder what Miriam would say to us if she could tell us about this time in her life."* I say this in almost a musing manner, and I let the silence hang a bit, see whether a head comes up or whether anyone takes the cue. Then making my question fully direct: *"Would anyone like to speak for a moment as Miriam? Tell us, Miriam, what is this time like for you?"* Here in slight shifts I move from the indirect (I wonder what Miriam would say . . .) to the direct (Tell us, Miriam, what this time is like for you).

Worst case (I have never seen it happen, but it is our fear): no one speaks.

Then you as the director might wish to offer your own speculation as *Miriam*. You might begin saying, "Well, I think Miriam might say the following if she were here to tell us her story:

'This is a cruel time for me. I am caught between impossible choices. On the one hand, I cherish this little baby. On the other hand, his every cry threatens my life and those of my brother and mother and father.'"

Then you might say, "I wonder if there is another Miriam here who might have something else, or something different, to tell us?" You hope that your words have primed the pump. But let's say that, again, no one picks up on it. The silence that greets you may be the silence of resistance, but it also may be a silence which is suddenly filling with the enormity of that family's life. With no one else willing to play at that moment, you let go of the game, perhaps with some words like "Well, it was just a thought to talk to Miriam, to imagine her words; it's a kind of midrash. Maybe we will try it again some time." And you go on with the study session. You have planted a seed.

More likely, someone does respond to your invitation, or does offer a variant Miriam to the one you proposed. "I think Miriam would be scared," someone offers.

Hearing this, you notice that the phrasing is still indirect (Miriam would be afraid instead of I, as Miriam, am afraid). Your task here is to shift it into direct speech: "So, you are Miriam, and you are scared," you say gently, moving the participant into the role.

"Well, yes," perhaps with a slight shrug or a nervous laugh. Where is this going? This is different.

"And why are you scared?" you ask, persisting, but in a tone that is caring rather than confrontational. Students, adults perhaps more than young people, are so used to thinking there is a right answer, that even in a method so evidently open and imaginative as this one, students may still feel cornered by any interrogation. You take the role of the concerned friend rather than probing director.

"Well, she's scared be . . . ."

"I'm scared because . . . ," insisting gently that the role be played.

"All right, I'm scared because this little baby could get us all in trouble. In big trouble."

"Yes," I say, and echoing "My parents broke the law, and we are living in whispers. Is that right?" referring back to the participant.

"Yes, I mean, what if he were discovered? What if it were found out that we were hiding him?"

"What could happen?"

"We could get into big trouble."

"Ah hah. Like . . . ?"

"I don't know. I don't want to think about it. All I know is that we have to be very secret, very quiet. Like you said 'whispers.'"

"It's hard," I say.

"Yes, it's very hard. Any day they could come and search our house; they could find us out."

"Thank you," I say to this participant. "So, perhaps this is one of the things Miriam might tell us if she could speak to us today." And I see how the class wishes to move from this point.

"You know, I never thought of Anne Frank before, but in some ways this Miriam, or maybe it's the baby Moses, reminds me of her."

"In what way?" I ask.

"You know, hidden, hiding, scared." And we smoothly resume our other ways of talking about the story.

5. Bibliodrama with Talking Objects

Certain schools of modern dream interpretation suggest that the best way to understand a dream is to imagine that we are every part of it, not just the dream-self or dream-protagonist. We are all the other characters as well, and we are also the dream's images, objects, plots, and relationships. It makes perfect sense, of course, since it is our mind that spins out the dream web in all its detail. I find this perspective useful in freeing me to think of objects as having consciousness, and in this regard it is not hard for me to think of the Bible as God's dream within which everything has meaning and a charge of life. I often use these analogies as a way of warming-up a class or a group to a bibliodramatic exercise in which we find a voice for objects in the Bible and have them speak to us.

Here, for example, is a warm-up that I have used with moderate sized groups (under twelve) when I want to hear from — or at least open up the possibility of hearing from — everyone in the group. I offer my words in italics to show what it is I might actually say:

The Bible is full of objects: stones, swords, wells, mountains, staffs, arks of different kind. You get the idea. Think of an object in the Exodus story that interests you, or perhaps one that just pops into your head for no good reason that you can see. Raise your hand when you have such a object in mind. (I proceed in this fashion so that people make a commitment to an object without having to think about having to speak for it.) Now imagine you are that object. Introduce yourself to us in the following way: "I am Moses' staff." If you are not comfortable with this exercise, please feel free just to watch and listen.

Most of the members of the group in turn — some with a smile, some with a giggle, many without much expression, some with a certain playfulness — introduce themselves in this manner.

"I am the staff God gives to Moses."

"I am the frog on Pharaoh's bed."

"I am the whip of the Egyptian taskmaster."

"I am the little reed ark that carried Moses down the Nile."

"I am the burning bush."

"I am the angel of death in the 10th Plague."

The exercise gains momentum and energy as it proceeds. We feel that these objects have stories to tell. And part of the virtue of choosing an object rather than a character for this exercise is that the object's story is often more focused in a particular narrative moment. The task of the facilitator, depending on the time available, is to elicit some of these stories.

So as a next step one might ask: "Do any of you wish to tell us anything about yourself?" Here is an example of what I heard a woman say in an adult Torah group:

"I am the reed ark that carried Moses down the Nile."

"Tell me more about yourself."

"Well, what do you want to know?"

"Who made you."

"I don't know." (This response is not at all unusual and represents an important and challenging moment for the facilitator. The participant is, for a moment, caught in a dilemma. It is not yet clear whether she can give full rein to her imagination, making up a story out of whole cloth, or whether she has to adhere to the information — or lack thereof — in the Bible. The task of the facilitator at this point is to encourage imagination to invent the story).

"Well, someone must have made you, and though your story is not told in the Bible, perhaps you can let us in on some of your secrets." Or, "I know we do not know in a factual way anything about you, but in this exercise you are free to make up a story. I'll ask you a few questions, and you can just see what answers come to mind." Or, "Sure you know. Maybe you're afraid you'll get them into trouble, that the Egyptian authorities will trace your story and arrest those who arranged for Moses' escape. Don't

worry; none of us here will reveal a word of what you tell us." The important thing here is, in the spirit of play and invention, to encourage the role-player to let her imagination respond.

"OK. Moses' father made it."

"Made me," I say, gently correcting the speaker back into role.

"OK. Made me."

"Did he talk to you while he was making you?"

"Not actually aloud."

"But you could read his thoughts?"

"Not his thoughts, his feelings."

"Ah hah. And what were those feelings?"

"He was sad, and he was angry."

"I see. And did you know what you were being made for?"

"Yes."

"And that was?"

"To carry the little infant down the Nile."

"How did you feel about this assignment?"

"It was a huge responsibility. I wanted Moses' father to be very careful. To weave me well and to caulk me well. I did not want to leak, or tilt over."

"And did he build you well?"

"Yes, very well."

"Yes. I want you to know what it felt like to carry him down the river. It was like being his mother."

"Ah hah. If I understand you, you are saying . . ." (and here I echo) "I was like a second mother to Moses."

"Yes, a second womb. I held him safe and warm. I rocked him gently. I whispered to him. And I was the one who gave him his name."

"And that name is . . . ?"

"Moshe . . . it means 'the one who is drawn out.'"

"Out of . . . ?"

"Out of me."

"How important you were."

"Yes. And I was sad to let him go, but I had done what I was made to do, and I was glad. But then I was empty."

"Well, thank you for sharing your story."

Another way of working with objects, is to arrange the objects in various ways, for example, the frogs and the staff have a conversation. Objects may then share a story or sense their relationship with other objects. Interesting juxtapositions open up surprising interpretations; conversations between objects are full of insight, humor, and pathos. In the course of the exercise participants discover how connected they are to these objects; through them they are able to question, quarrel, comment on the story in which they are embedded.

6. The Encounter: Dramatic Dialogue

The encounter — eye to eye, hand to hand — is the heart of the western dramatic imagination. Encounters are not necessarily hostile; but they are charged, layered, and human, the point and counterpoint of differing voices, the meeting face to face of differing perspectives. The biblical imagination is also drawn to such scenes of encounter; we find them everywhere, like Moses and Pharaoh, yet we can imagine dramatic dialogues that are never actually repeated in the Bible. For example, ask two people to role-play Moses' biological mother and Pharaoh's daughter — his adoptive mother.

7. Posting

Posting (with its embedded Latin preposition post meaning after) refers to everything that happens from the end of the action phase through the closure of the bibliodramatic event. In and during posting no one should speak any further in role; to do so would be by definition to go back into action.

Always one wants to leave time at the end for posting. Participants and observers need a chance to comment on the process, to share what the experience has been like, what they learned. It may be surprising how much excitement this simple, safe exercise generates.

In the closure to the class where the woman played the reed ark, she expressed her surprise at how vivid the scene had become for her. "I really see Moses' father bending over in candlelight and weaving the basket. It was amazing, and as the basket I had feelings, too. It was harder to say Goodbye to the baby than I said."

And another group member, speaking to her, said, "I never thought about the ark before as a kind of second mother, a womb. I mean I guess it's obvious, but it made me realize how many times Moses was mothered and passed on. The little ark is like a metaphor for how transient his childhood must have felt for him."

Though these comments have a degree of adult sophistication, this exercise lends itself well to young kids, to families, and particularly intergenerational groups. Kids may not have the same ability to comment on the objects as adults, but they are far less inhibited in representing them in the first place. I'll never forget the kid who, playing Joseph's coat, said, "It was scary when the brothers tore me into pieces and splashed blood on me. They were so mad. Like wolves."

A rabbi once said of this work that it created "a level playing field." What he meant was that this method does not privilege knowledge or book-learning. As a result it is possible for men and women, boys and girls, of all ages and familiarities with the Bible to enter into a midrashic community together in which what is valued is imagination, empathy, and certain expressive abilities.

[*Editor:* To identify with the biblical story and to retell it dramatically is a survival skill for Jewish continuity.]

Chronicles

"All the News That's Fit to Print"

News of the Past

DR. ISRAEL ELDAD, Editor   GOSHEN, 25 Kislev (1270 B.C.E.)

Pharaoh's Daughter Stands By Her "Son"

(Chronicles News Service)

Rameses, 21 Tybi. – A surprising statement in defense of Moses was made today by Bint-Anat, Pharaoh Rameses' favorite daughter (and for ten years now, his wife), when she learned of what her adopted son had done.

There was great excitement in and around the Queen's palace today after the publication of the official announcement about the murder of Mai and the identity of the murderer.

Palace guards refused admittance to reporters who wanted to interview Bint-Anat. But to everyone's surprise, the Queen herself appeared on her balcony and called out to the crowd gathered below: "I am proud of my son Moses for being loyal to his people and for refusing to suffer injustice!"

Hebrew Leaders Condemn Murder of Overseer

Influential Hebrew clan chiefs condemned the deed as "irresponsible." Korach said: "We must aid the authorities in their search for the killer. If we demonstrate our loyalty to Pharaoh, perhaps he will not pour out his wrath upon the Hebrew population."

'PRINCE' MOSES IS A HEBREW!

ACCUSED OF SLAYING EGYPTIAN OFFICIAL, HE FLEES EGYPT

POLICE CONTINUE SEARCH

MOSES SLAYS OVERSEER MAI, as depicted by our artist

STOP PRESS!!

Early this morning, the fugitive Moses crossed the Egyptian border and headed for the wilderness. It is believed here in Goshen, that Moses will seek a haven in Midian as a political refugee. The Midianites are racially related to the Abraham Clan.

(Chronicle News Service)

RAMESES, 22 Tybi. – Moses, adopted son of the Queen of Egypt, is the man who killed the Egyptian overseer, Mai, in Pithom two days ago.

This startling revelation was made last night in a special announcement released by the Royal Palace. Even more surprising is the fact, revealed in the announcement, that Moses is of Hebrew stock – and is not an Egyptian, as was generally believed until now.

The perpetrator of the slaying, says the official statement, is presently in hiding, but the police are continuing their search for him. Unofficial reports say Moses has fled the country.

Mai, son of Bakenamos – the murdered man – was Chief Overseer of Public Works. Two days ago he came to Pithom on a tour of inspection. Dissatisfied, apparently, with the tempo of the work at one particular spot, Mai summoned the Hebrew foreman, a man named Carmi.

Beaten Unconscious

Before Carmi could open his mouth, Mai assailed the hapless supervisor with his copper-headed staff, beating him viciously about the head and shoulders until his victim dropped to the ground, unconscious. The Hebrew slaves – there were about

Continued on Page 42, Column 4

Chronicles

founded in 1541 B.C.E.

An Appeal to Moses

Like a flash of lightning on a dark and dreary night, *the man* came and went – and for a moment lit up the gloomy skies of Goshen. He did not grow up in our midst; he never felt the sting of the whip, the ignominy of slavery. Nevertheless, he frequently left the splendor of the royal palace to join his brethren and was profoundly moved by the bitterness of their fate – not just by the physical pain they suffer, but equally by the spiritual degradation to which they are subjected.

Two days ago he acted. He killed an Egyptian overseer who had been wantonly beating a Hebrew slave. When he struck down that Egyptian slave-driver, he was fully prepared to take upon himself the responsibility for his act. But now Moses has fled. And from what has been learned from his brother Aaron, it was not from the Egyptians that he fled.

No, Moses did not flee from the Egyptians. He fled from us – his own brethren. Many of us grumbled about the attack on the Egyptian overseer. Worse than that: Some even hurried to the authorities and revealed to them the identity of the man who had killed the Egyptian.

It was a bitterly disillusioned Moses who yesterday left Egypt and us. We are not yet worthy of redemption.

But we appeal to Moses: Listen to us!

We do not believe you will be able to stay away from us very long. You may succeed in fleeing from Goshen and from Egypt, but we doubt very much that you will be able to flee from the flame that burns within you. That flame will go on burning, and it will leave you no rest.

Remember it and come back to your people. And we hope that when you do, you will know not only how to straighten our bent backs, our enslaved bodies, but also how to free our spirit from the shackles that bind it today.

Bint-Anat Popular with Israelites

By OUR CORRESPONDENT

Queen Bint-Anat found her way to the hearts of Goshen's Hebrew population long before it became know that Moses, her adopted son, was a Hebrew. It is an open secret that on her account only was the dread decree ordering the drowning of Hebrew male infants abolished.

Likewise, it was her intervention which prevented her father-husband from extending his forced-labor program to the Israelite women. The Children of Israel have gone so far as to rename the Queen "Batya" – "Daughter of God" – rather than Bint-Anat which means "daughter of the goddess Anat."

Egypt In The Eyes Of A Stranger

Sir:

I am an Ugarit merchant, and I have been in Egypt for 6 months, on business. I am in a position to say that Egypt has a black future ahead of her.

Wherever I turn, I see foreigners. There seem to be more Hebrews, Canaanites, Libyans, and Sardinians here than there are Egyptians! Can a kingdom be built upon that kind of foundation? Suppose these Hebrew slaves should take it into their heads one day to flee the country; or suppose the foreign merchants should decide, for some reason or other, to take their business elsewhere; or suppose all these foreign mercenaries in the Egyptian army should become dissatisfied with their pay and turn on their Egyptians officers. I venture to predict that if any of these eventualities – or, indeed, a combination of them – should come to pass, this whole lopsided structure that is the modern Egyptian state will topple to the ground.

Avibaal

Murder of Mai: We'll Have To Pay

Sir:

Together with the rest of the Children of Israel, we were profoundly shocked by the killing of the Egyptian, Mai. Only now that the murderer has been identified do we understand the real meaning of Jacob's curse on Simon and Levi: ". . . For in their fury they slew a man . . . ." (Gen. 49).

Our fury is upon you, too, the editors of *Chronicles*. How is it you did not at once denounce the murder – even though it was not known at first who was its perpetrator?

And now that the murderer is known, let us ask: Who gave him the authority to punish, or the command to avenge? Who gave him permission to lay hands on an Egyptian official? This foul deed stands in direct contradiction to the spirit of our ancestors, who preferred to suffer in silence rather than engage in bloodshed.

Anyway, no matter what the rights or wrongs of the case, no matter what the principles involved, one very practical result is certain to come out of this whole sordid mess: We Hebrews are going to be made to pay for it – with our sweat and our blood!

Datan and Aviram

400 Years?

Sir:

The God of our Fathers told Abraham that we should be slaves for 400 years. It seems to me we had better accept our fate in silence and not try to rush things. Precipitate action such as that taken by Moses can only make a bad situation worse.

Palti Ben Raphu Benjamin

'PRINCE' MOSES IS A HEBREW

continued from page 1

800 of them on this site – continued toiling all this time, not daring to look up, even for a moment, from their labors.

Mai left after having appointed a successor to Carmi and having ordered him to see to it that no aid was extended to the injured man. The overseer completed his round of inspection before dark and left Pithom in his chariot, driving alone.

He never reached home. According to information received later by the police, Mai's chariot was stopped, some distance from Pithom, by a man wearing the garb of an Egyptian officer.

Moses' Sister Under Arrest

(Chronicle News Service)

Miriam, sister of Moses, was arrested at her home last night and taken to Rameses, the capital, for questioning. The authorities suspect her of having been in contact with her brother, both before and after the murder, and of having helped him to escape.

Miriam admitted under questioning, that she frequented the Queen's palace in Rameses. But there has never been any secret about this. She has long been a well-known figure at the palace, where she was authorized to give the women music and dancing lessons.

Mother Confident, Father Silent

"The God of our ancestors, who saved my son from death in the Nile, will continue to protect him and will save him from the sword of Pharaoh, as well," said Yocheved, Moses' aged mother, last night.

Amram, Moses's father, declined to make any statement whatsoever. He seemed disturbed and bewildered by what had transpired.

Surprise in Goshen

By a Staff Writer

Word of Moses' Hebrew origin spread rapidly through the province of Goshen yesterday, in the wake of the announcement from the Palace. Everyone exhibited genuine surprise, although one frequently heard such remarks as: "Come to think of it, Moses has been acting peculiarly of late"!

Witnessed Flogging

For a number of weeks now Moses has been paying daily visits to the work sites in Goshen. It was generally assumed that this "Egyptian prince" was being groomed for a supervisory post at one of these sites. But Moses behaved rather strangely for a taskmaster.

Unlike the other Egyptian overseers, Moses was in the habit of entering into conversation with the slaves and, stranger still, lending them a helping hand occasionally! In spite of his unusual conduct, however, no one suspected that Moses was himself a Hebrew.

On the day of the slaying, Moses was seen in the vicinity of the spot where the Israelite foreman, Carmi, was flogged by the Egyptian overseer, Mai.

The assassination of Mai had one very noticeable effect on the Egyptian force of supervisors: The following day (yesterday) not one of them raised a hand against a Hebrew slave. The Israelite foremen, on the other hand, exhibited a marked tendency toward greater strictness.

Datan, of the tribe of Reuben, was particularly harsh in his treatment of the men who worked under him. Moses came up on him yesterday just as he was about to settle with his stick, an argument he was having with one of the workers. Moses at once intervened, staying the hand of the aggressive foreman.

Veiled Threat

Datan's reply gave Moses a severe shock. "Who made you a prince and a judge over us"? he challenged Moses. "Perhaps you intend to kill me – as you killed the Egyptian!"

You deserve a factual look at . . .

Myths about Egypt and the 'Hebrews'
Who are these so-called 'Hebrews' anyway?

We all know that, by dint of constant repetition, white can be made to appear black, good can get misinformed into evil, and myth may take the place of reality. Egypt, with roughly one-hundredth of the world's population and a similar fraction of the territory of the planet, has been vilified throughout the world for allegedly holding the "Hebrews" in "slavery." It's time you had a look at the facts.

What are the facts?

Myth: The "Hebrews" are a nation and therefore deserving of freedom.
Reality: The concept of Hebrew nationhood is a new one, raised entirely by outside agitators. The so-called "Hebrews" are nothing more than a wandering tribe of desert nomads. They are no more different from the Canaanites, Hittites, and Emorites than a Heliopolite is different from Memphan.
Myth: The "Hebrews" have a legitimate religion and should be allowed to practice it.
Reality: This alleged Hebrew religion is, again, entirely a new invention. It might better be characterized as a cult: they claim that there is only one god, who has chosen them as his special people, and promised them an ill-defined territory to boot. We must add that the concept that a slave religion, the religion of a loser, is deserving of respect from an empire such as ours, is truly something new in human history.
Myth: The "Hebrews" will be satisfied with a few days in the wilderness to sacrifice to their god.
Reality: Their cult is in fact highly dangerous. Clearly, they would attempt an escape if allowed to leave for a few days. And then what? Their "god" has supposedly promised them the land of Canaan — but can anyone really believe that they will be satisfied with Canaan? If we let them go, we will have created a powerful adversary on our doorstep.
Myth: We owe the Hebrews something because of Joseph.
Reality: Who was this "Joseph"? We do not know "Joseph."
Myth: We keep them in slavery, make their lives harsh.
Reality: How dare they call this slavery! They live under Egyptian law — remember that they came here, a weary band of desert stragglers on the verge of starvation, and we rescued them. In return, they must accept the rule of our law: as Pharaoh needs you, you work. Most Egyptians work on these projects too!

They are well-fed, with hardly a care in the world. They are fat, indulged, over-sexed. In fact, their population has grown so much that we have had to institute mild population control measures — hardly what you would expect in a "slave" population "oppressed so hard they could not stand."

Should they ever achieve freedom in the wilderness, it will be but a few weeks before they are rebelling and whining about how good life was in Egypt.
Myth: The "Hebrews" are a peaceful group and will give us no trouble.
Reality: They are terrorists, nothing more. Remember the recent incident where a Hebrew terrorist murdered an Egyptian foreman in cold blood? *Not one* Hebrew "leader" has stepped forward to denounce this act of terrorism.

This ad has been published and paid for by

Friends of Law and Pharaoh

FLAP is a tax-exempt, non-profit organization. Its purpose is research and publication of facts regarding developments in Egypt and exposing false propaganda that might harm the interests of the Pharaoh and his allies.

Yes, I want to help in the publication of these ads in defense of Pharaoh. Here is my contribution.

Name _____

Title _____

Son of _____

of (city) _____

Send to FLAP, Palace of Pharaoh, Qantir, Lower Egypt

7

My Personal Exodus
The Inner Journey from Slavery to Liberation: Egypt and Exodus as Metaphors for Personal Growth

■ by Joel Ziff

"The Exodus from Egypt occurs in every human being, in every era, in every year and even in every day."
— *Rabbi Nachman of Bratzlav (Ukraine, 19th C.)*

The liberation from slavery in Egypt marks the birth of the Jewish nation. **The event serves not only as a marker of turning points in the development of the Jewish people; it is also symbolic of critical moments in our lives.** For this reason, we read in the Hagaddah, that "each of us is obligated to consider ourselves as coming out of Egypt." The coming out of Egypt is an archetypal image of life transitions. It embodies every narrow passage we traverse as we give birth to ourselves: leaving home, career changes, marriage, divorce, birth, sickness, death, addiction, and recovery from trauma. Each of us has journeyed into our own Egypt and each of us struggles to achieve a personal Exodus.

A. *Turning Crisis into Opportunity: Slavery in Egypt as a Positive Transformative Experience*

The inevitable difficulties of life can overwhelm us, leaving us defeated, hopeless, and depressed. If we view these experiences solely as oppressive events, we find ourselves enslaved in Egypt and unable to escape. The stress can destroy our will, our energy, and our capacity to respond constructively. The story of slavery in Egypt offers us a different possibility: the Israelites not only overcome the adversity; they develop into a nation. Viewing our lives through the mirror of the Israelites' experience, we may be

Dr. Joel Ziff *is a psychotherapist in Boston. This is a selection from his forthcoming* Mirrors in Time: A Psycho-Spiritual Journey through the Jewish Year, *Jason Aronson Publishers*

able to envision a similar outcome for ourselves in which we not only overcome difficulties, but develop new capacities in the process.

This theme of opportunity in adversity is repeated again in the story of the Israelites' initial migration to Egypt. Jacob's sons became jealous of their brother Joseph and sold him into slavery. Joseph was taken to Egypt. He predicted a famine and developed a plan to store grain and avoid disaster. When the famine struck, Jacob's sons came to Egypt and were saved by Joseph. Joseph did not resent his brothers or punish them. Instead, he reminded them that their misdeed ultimately produced a positive outcome, saving the Israelites from the famine: *"Do not be angry with yourselves that you sold me, for God sent me before you to preserve life."* (GENESIS 45:5)

Sometimes birth does not occur willingly. We are freed despite ourselves. Perhaps current resistances can be understood as resistance to freedom, viewed as birth pains rather than ordinary suffering and misery.

B. *Symbols of Transformation*

"Egypt" is associated with three metaphors: the **womb**, the **soil** in which a seed is planted, and a smelting **furnace**. The "exodus" from Egypt is seen as the journey through the birth canal, the sprouting of a seed (spring holiday), and the creation of a strong metal in the smelting furnace. The mirrors provided by these images and symbols allow us to see ourselves in a new way.

Exodus from Egypt as a Birth

The Hebrew word for Egypt, *Mitzrayim*, means narrow place. The Hassidic rebbe, Shneur Zalman suggests an association with the narrowness of the womb. Just as Egypt offered sanctuary to the seventy souls of Jacob's family who fled the famine in Canaan, so the womb offers sustenance, warmth, and protection to the fetus. As the fetus reaches full term, the once nurturing womb becomes oppressive. In the same way, as Jacob's family prospered and grew, Egypt was transformed into a place of servitude. The image of the splitting of the sea is suggestive of the breaking of the waters which occurs just before birth. The exodus becomes the passage through the birth canal.

The journey through these straits cannot be accomplished without outside intervention. The Israelites could not mobilize to fight their oppressors; they could only cry out in their suffering.

Similarly, the growing fetus, pushing the limits of the womb, initiates the birth process, but must rely on external forces to make the journey through the birth canal, a process that takes great effort. The newborn infant is dependent and powerless; a baby cannot survive independently. The infant needs a parent who accepts the powerlessness and vulnerability, who offers unconditional support and nurturance.

As we view our lives through the mirror of this image, we can validate our ability to recognize and express our pain. We can also acknowledge our powerlessness. We learn to accept our resistance to the birth of a new aspect of self. We focus on sources of unconditional support, both spiritual and material, which help us through the crisis.

Egypt as a Smelting Furnace

In the Torah, Egypt is also described through analogy to a smelting furnace: *"But God has taken you out of the iron furnace, out of Egypt to be a people of inheritance, as you are this day."* (DEUTERONOMY 4:20) In a smelting furnace, raw metal is exposed to extreme heat. As it melts, impurities are separated and the now liquid metal can be mixed with other materials to create a new, stronger substance. It can be shaped and molded for a variety of purposes. Correspondingly, the heat and fire of oppression produces a transformation: impurities are separated and removed, so that the remaining essence can be mixed to shape the Israelites for their higher work.

The image of the smelting furnace offers another mirror for making sense of our experience. The fire of crisis is no longer a destructive force. In the heat of the fire of crisis, the old Ego melts, the impurity within ourselves can similarly be removed, and the Essence can be reshaped.

C. Stages in the Process of Redemption

One commentator asks why God, who is omnipotent, did not simply take the Jews immediately from Egypt. What was the need for responding to the resistance by Pharaoh with plagues and other miracles? Why bother with all of these intermediary steps instead of resolving the issue quickly and directly? If the only issue was oppression, God could have acted more efficiently. However, the material oppression left its mark spiritually and emotionally, scarring the souls of the Israelites.

They needed to confront the interjected slave mentality, not just leave the land of oppression. The plagues and the various stages in the journey to freedom are important insofar as the Israelites are transformed in the process.

D. Applying the Images of Pesach to Our Lives: An Old Self and New Circumstances

The journey of the children of Israel to Egypt began as an effort to escape the famine in the land of Israel. Egypt provided nurturance for many years. But then, a new Pharaoh came to power, one who "did not know Joseph." (EXODUS 1:8) The circumstances changed. What had been a place of nurturance became a place of slavery. The children of Israel suffered but were unable to extricate themselves. Only with divine intervention could they free themselves. Once they left Egypt, they found themselves in the desert, a new environment with different circumstances. Although they were free, they had no sources of food and water: they lacked the structure which shaped their lives. The mentality of the slave no longer provided a useful identity which could enable them to survive and grow.

We see ourselves in the mirror of the story of the redemption from slavery in Egypt. Each of us journeys to our own Egypt, as a way to respond to a threat or to address a need. We identify how we may be trapped and enslaved in our lives so as to begin our own process of liberation. As we grow and develop, our needs change. We find ourselves constricted in some way. Initially, we may fail to notice that a problem exists. We may not be aware of other possibilities; we may deaden ourselves to our dissatisfaction; we may not understand the true cause of difficulties we do experience; or, we may be afraid that change is not possible.

The process of redemption begins with awareness; the awareness that one is enslaved and suffering fuels the determination and the wish to change. When did the Israelites notice their enslavement? Was it when their working conditions deteriorated? Was it when the decree was made to kill all male infants? We remind ourselves of this suffering when we eat maror, the bitter herbs at the seder. As we identify with the pain of our ancestors, we become more aware of our own condition, of how we are also enslaved and powerless. We may cry out in our pain but not know the cause or the solution.

As we experience the suffering of our condition and our inability to make changes in it, we begin to cry out for help.

Often, we may criticize ourselves for "breaking down" or for failing to act more independently. The crying out of the Israelites provides a more constructive image. When we cry out for help, we are beginning to reconnect with the Essence of life, with the Self or with God, with the *Nitzotz* (the divine spark) within ourselves.

We begin to address the problem only when something happens to push us out of the old structure of our lives, forcing us into a new environment. The miracle of the Ten Plagues is an important image because it reminds us that external forces in the universe can help us even when we are unable to help ourselves. These miracles help us trust that the universe can be powerful, compassionate, and supportive.

We can easily make the mistake of imagining that the experience of liberation is one of joy and relief. However, liberation is often stressful and filled with uncertainty. The Hebrews struggled with their anxiety, uncertain whether to oppose Pharaoh. This reminds us that our own liberation also may be stressful and that we may be ambivalent about change. The story of the Splitting of the Sea provides an archetypal image of the struggle we experience as we disconnect from the old identity.

It is only after the miracle of the Splitting of the Sea that Moses, Miriam, and the children of Israel, for the first time, sing praises of gratitude to God. Until this moment, the Israelites were skeptical. They did not believe they could escape Pharaoh's oppression. With the miracle of the sea, they realize that liberation is possible. In this same way, we experience joy as we are freed; we experience the freedom of choice rather than compulsion.

An Activity for the Seder: Sharing Our Internal Struggles to Achieve "Exodus"

Some groups of friends have developed an introspective seder in which they are willing to share within the table-community their inner journeys. They ask each participant to reflect on their own "Egypt," the constraining aspects in their personal lives, and to describe it briefly at the seder. Then they share their personal "Exodus," transformations in their lives which even though painful, have liberated new forces for self-growth.

You may wish to copy Joel Ziff's article and mail it to the participants in advance. Ask them to prepare a little card which says: "My Personal Egypt is _____" and to think about the forces allowing or compelling them to undergo an Exodus to a new world.

At the seder invite a few people to share their "Egypts" and their "Exoduses." Allow those who do not wish to share their experiences to "pass." Try to avoid "heavy" psychological sessions, but let the analogy of psychological and historical slavery and liberation percolate through the discussion.

≈ Chapter 8
Recalling Great Seders and Great Exoduses of the Past

In *A Different Night* we suggested the participants might want to recall special seders that they have experienced, just as we all recall and reenact the original Egyptian seder (1200 B.C.E.).

The traditional Haggadah mentions the famous all night seder of the five Rabbis in Bnai Brak which may be related to their involvement in Judea's battle for freedom against the Roman Empire (early 2nd century C.E.). Similarly one may recall seders at other important junctures in history in which the discussion of Egyptian slavery provided a forum for confronting contemporary issues of oppression.

- The First Passover in Eretz Yisrael:
  Joshua at the Hill of Foreskins

- Marranos Observe Passover in Spain and Portugal,
  after 1492

- The "Seder" of Righteous Gentiles:
  A Family Commemoration of Liberation from the Nazis,
  The Netherlands, 1945

- Our First Seder in Israel: Soviet Jews, 1990

- The Exodus from Ethiopia:
  A Night of Terror and of Hope, 1991

- The Legendary Seder in Katmandu, 1991

- My Parents' Personal Passover Ritual,
  Contemporary U.S.A.

The First Pass-Over in Eretz Yisrael: Joshua at the Hill of Foreskins

Joshua's first Passover in Israel has much to teach us of Pesach as a rite of passage in Jewish history. In the month of Nisan exactly 40 years after the first seder in Egypt and the splitting of the Red Sea, God split the Jordan River and Joshua led the people into Eretz Yisrael. While the passage over the Jordan brook was hardly life threatening, it was symbolic of a deep change of geography and national character. The people of Israel passed from the desert to farm land, from a nomadic tribe to a nation state. It is no accident that this passage coincided with the first Pass-Over celebration in Israel and with the mass circumcision of all the males born in the desert.

At that time the LORD said to Joshua, *"Make flint knives and proceed with a second circumcision of the men of Israel at Givaat-haAralot, the Hill of the Foreskins."*

The LORD said to Joshua, *"Today I have rolled away from you the disgrace of Egypt."* So that place was [also] called Gilgal, 'Place of the Rolling Away . . . ."* (JOSHUA 5)

The "second circumcision" was in fact the first rite of passage for a generation born to freedom in the desert after their parents — born to slavery in Egypt — perished on the way to Canaan. The generation of the Exodus died off while serving a 40 year sentence of exile because they were too cowardly to fight for their place in the land of Canaan. Too easily panicked by the reports of 10 of the 12 spies, they rejected the land of milk and honey.

Now Joshua, their new political and military commander-in-chief, made his sword into a knife of ritual circumcision to induct all the males of his army and their children into the "bris" (covenant) of Abraham. In this act of male bonding, the disgrace of Egypt was rolled away and with it the historic

8

memories of servility in Egypt and of cowardice in the desert.

After the freshly circumcised generation partook of the Pesach lamb, they bid farewell to manna and celebrated the fruitfulness of their new land. Joshua's mass circumcision was a covenant that both "cuts" and "binds." The new generation cut its umbilical cords with the slave generation and bound itself together as a fighting brotherhood newly tied to its land. Dependence — whether on Pharaoh's malevolent will or on Divine beneficence in the desert — was replaced by a newly won self-reliance.

The Marranos Observe Passover in Spain and Portugal, after 1492

■ *Hayyim Schauss*

At the end of the European Middle Ages there evolved a notable method of observing Pesach among the Marranos, the secret Jews of Spain and Portugal. These Marranos were entirely separated from Jews and from Jewish life. They had no Jewish books, and the only book on which they could draw for rules of Jewish life was the Latin Bible of the Catholic Church. They tried to live, not as the Jews of their day did, but as the Jews of the time of the Kings and the Prophets. They knew nothing of the development of Pesach through the ages.

The question arises: How did these Marranos, who had no Jewish calendars and no contacts with other Jews, know when to observe the various Jewish festivals? Actually, they did not; they reckoned the Jewish holidays by the calendar in general use, applying the Jewish days to the secular month. Thus they observed Yom Kippur on the tenth day after the New Moon of September and Pesach at the full moon of March. When the spies of the Inquisition discovered these observances, the Marranos of Spain postponed the dates of the festivals, observing Yom Kippur on the eleventh day following the New Moon of September and celebrating the seder on a Pesach eve that came sixteen days after the appearance of the New Moon of March, instead of fourteen days.

On this sixteenth day they would bake their *matzot*; on the two preceding days which, according to their curious Jewish-secular calendar, were really Pesach, they ate neither bread nor *matzot*. There was no ceremony of the burning of the *chametz*. Instead they burned a piece of dough prepared for the baking of

the *matzot*. In the evening they observed a secret seder in their homes, eating an entire roast sheep, all the participants wearing their traveling shoes and bearing staves in their hand, exactly as described in the Bible. There were even Marranos, those of Mexico, who followed the old biblical injunction to smear the blood of the sheep on their doorposts.

One noteworthy custom grew up among these Marranos: the custom of beating the waters of a stream with willow branches, which they interpreted as a reminder of the separating of the waters of the Red Sea. The Pesach of the Marranos is not entirely a thing of the past. There are, to this very day, Marranos in Portugal who still observe Pesach in the manner just described.

Splitting the Red 'Puddle' in Belmonte, Portugal

■ *Paul Cowan (journalist, author of* An Orphan in History*)*

Hallel sings of God's redemption of Israel at the Red Sea, but during many periods of persecution the Jews have not always been able to praise our God in public. Since the 1490's in Portugal, the forced conversions and the Inquisition have prevented the Jews called "conversos" or Marranos from celebrating Passover. To preserve some shreds of tradition, the Jews invented an alternative Pesach liturgy to be conducted either in cellars or in the mountains. These new traditions have been preserved for 500 years until today. A contemporary journalist describes them:

"Once, during Passover week, small groups of 'conversos' meet for a picnic in the mountains. Afterward, dressed in white, they gather by a brook or even a puddle. They carry olive branches, beat the surface of the water, and pretend it parts as the Red Sea did for Moses. Then, they cross it, to symbolize Moses' crossing out of Egypt. On the other side, they stand together, waving their olive branches, and sing their Passover prayer for freedom:

'On the 14th day of the moon
Of the first month of the year
The people leave Egypt
(and go to the shores of the Red Sea).
When will you bring us, Moses,
Out of this empty land (Portugal)
Where there is no bread, no wood?
Here comes Moses with his staff.

He beats the sea.
The sea has opened up in 13 places
My people will surely pass [the 12 tribes and the priests].
The way the Lord commanded.
Let us praise the Lord, who is our God!'"

The "Seder" of Righteous Gentiles: A Family Commemoration of Liberation, The Netherlands, 1945

When Emperor Napoleon invaded Russia in the early 1800's, his military government forced all citizens to take last names. In Augustova near Minsk, one Jewish family was called into the military office to pick a last name immediately after Tisha B'Av, the day when Jews remember the destruction of the First and Second Temples. They had just been to the synagogue where they prayed and wept as they remembered the destruction of Zion, the poetic name for Jerusalem. So this family chose the last name — "Zion." In 1856, the Zion family left Russia and settled in Holland, in a village called Eibergen, where they opened a clothing store.

In 1940, the Germans invaded Holland. In 1941, the Jews of Holland were ordered by the German Nazis to report for "re-settlement." The Zion family had three brothers and three sisters who decided to go underground. Even though Jews had little social contact with their Calvinist Protestant neighbors, Jews were helped by the ministers of the Calvinist church, Puritans who helped organize the underground movement.

Even before the war, one of the Dutch ministers would go across the border from Holland to Germany to try to convince the German Calvinists to oppose the Nazis. Soon, the German ministers, who wanted to prove their loyalty to the Nazis, refused to allow him to speak at their services. After the Nazis invaded Holland, this minister, who was called Fritz "de Zwerver" (Fritz the Wanderer), would go from church to church in Holland on his bicycle. Since all rubber had been confiscated by the Germans, his bike had wooden wheels.

One Sunday morning Fritz arrived in Eibergen and walked to the podium of the Protestant church (the most important part of the Calvinist service was the sermon preached from the Bible). Even though there were pro-Nazi Dutch officials sitting in the front row, he opened his Bible to Exodus 1:15-22 and read the story of the midwives in Egypt who saved the Hebrew male children from drowning. Then he said to the congregation, "Who is the Pharaoh today? The Nazis! Who are the babies who have to be hidden? The Jews! Who are the midwives today? We are! It is our job to outsmart the Pharaohs, to have the courage of the midwives and to protect the Jews and all those being persecuted." Then he got on his bicycle and went to the next village. The people were inspired by Fritz de Zwerver, who encouraged them to organize an underground. Many members of the church participated, and hid Jews in their houses. Dutch architecture emphasizes large roofs on houses, where Jews and other refugees who went into hiding were placed — *under the roof* (*ondergedoken*).

During this period, Sallie Zion was hidden by these righteous gentiles in 40 different places. When the person protecting him would say, "I can't hide you any more," and he would have to find another hiding place. Sometimes he was told ahead of time that they would have to leave in a day or a week. Then someone would come from the underground, usually at night, on a bicycle, take them to a safe house and hide them under the roof.

The last place Sallie Zion and his brother stayed was at the home of the Wassink family, who lived in a kind of large farmhouse on the outskirts of town. They could see people coming across the fields to the house, and so could be alerted when danger approached. Sallie and his brother were hidden under the roof, a triangular space about three feet by six feet. (Sallie Zion carved a poem he wrote on one of the beams from the roof.)

Since they were on the outskirts of the town, they did not need to hide during the day. They were able to help with the household tasks, but always stayed indoors. When necessary they would go up a rope ladder, which could be folded and pulled up. The ladder was hidden behind a large embroidered wall hanging, traditional in Calvinist homes. It was embroidered in Dutch with the Biblical words:

בָּרוּךְ אַתָּה בְּבֹאֶךָ וּבָרוּךְ אַתָּה בְּצֵאתֶךָ

Blessed are You when you come in and when you go out!

Hidden with Sallie Zion and his brother were two Jewish girls, 16 and 18 years old, a Russian pilot, a Canadian pilot and a British pilot, who had been shot down and taken in by the family. Also hidden was the family's oldest son, and a first cousin who had been called to work in a German factory and did not want to go. All were hidden in one very narrow area.

A couple of days before the liberation of northeastern Holland from the Nazis in March, 1945, a lookout for the Wassinks reported that 13 Nazis and two Dutch collaborators were approaching. Quickly all the illegals hid under the roof. In order to remove all signs of the hidden illegals, Mrs. Wassink cleared away extra cutlery and dishes. She turned to her eldest daughter, gave her the stolen ration cards used to purchase extra food and told her to hide them in the barn in an old stove. Then she turned to her ten-year-old son, Wim, and told him to go visit relatives, but not to run lest he arouse suspicion. As Wim nonchalantly twirled a stick in the air, the Nazis spotted him and told him to come with them into the house. Other Nazis were coming down a path where a large log had fallen. Each German had to step over the log, but one who had a big potbelly tripped and fell. Wim wanted to laugh, but had to keep it inside. When they brought the boy into the house, it was about 11 a.m. The Nazis searched the house. One of them came to the kitchen and saw a large, black pot on the stove. He turned to the mother and pointed to the big pot, saying "too much food." She stood up and held her two fingers forming "V" in a victory sign and said, "This big pot is enough for two days." (Incidentally, the iron pot contained a carrot stew whose orange color is the national color of the Dutch Queen, symbol of the resistance to the Nazi occupation.)

While the Nazis continued to search, the Wassinks sat down for lunch. In a Calvinist household, everyone sits down for their big meal at lunch, a prayer is said and the Bible is read. The prayer Mrs. Wassink recited in Dutch was "May the evil Nazis be struck by blindness, just as the evil people of the Biblical city of Sodom were struck by blindness when they came to molest the guests taken in by Lot." (GENESIS 19) The Nazis continued their search and even measured the inside and outside of the house to see if there was any unaccounted for space. However, they measured the length and not the width. The hiding place under the attic was luckily, in the width of the house. The Nazis even went to the attic with a lantern. It shone on the hidden people, but when the Nazi held the lantern and tried to look through a crack, the light of the lantern blinded him, so in a way, Mrs. Wassink's prayer came true.

Then one of the Germans took Wim to the pigsty. "We know there are people hiding here. If you don't tell us where, we will throw you in with the pigs." The boy thought, "Pigs are certainly better than Nazis." The soldier began beating him. He screamed. (His older brother, one of the people in hiding, got upset and wanted to run and help Wim. The Russian pilot, Alex, took a pillow and shoved it over the brother's head until he calmed down.) Wim did not reveal anything.

After the beating, Wim's mother turned to the officer and pointed to her son. "Look how you have beaten him! Look at his bloody nose!" The officer apologized and told the German who had beaten the child to go to the yard, pump some water and wash the child's face. Then the Nazi officer told the family they would have to leave their house. He put up a sign declaring the house off limits. At night the underground came to extricate the people hiding "under the roof" including Sallie Zion and several days later the Allies arrived and liberated Eibergen.

On Dutch liberation day, May 5, the Wassink clan and all those they helped like to get together. They pull out the old iron pot and sometimes eat carrot stew. The embroidery of "Blessed are You as you enter" (which once covered the rope ladder leading to the hideaway) hangs on the wall next to the framed yellowing Nazi poster instructing everyone that this house is off limits. Though after the war the old house itself was razed, a scale model was constructed (like a dollhouse) showing the secret spaces. The family sits together on those occasions and the younger members ask the elders to retell the story in detail, so that it shall never be forgotten.

In a way this annual get-together is their personal Passover complete with symbolic foods, and stories of courage and Divine help. It is an interesting coincidence that the Torah reports that Lot served his guests in Sodom matza and so the Rabbis say that the rescue of Lot and his endangered guests (in fact, angels) occurred on Pesach.

First Seder in Israel, Soviet Jews, 1990

■ *Felix and Valentina Kochubievsky,
Soviet Jewry activists, Jerusalem*

Door-to-Door Service

We'd been waiting 10 years to get out of the USSR and make aliyah to Israel. Our two sons had been granted exit visas when we applied as a family in May 1978, but we were refused for "government considerations." During the decade that we waited I'd become active in fighting the refusal policy and had served two and a half years in labor camp for my efforts. So when the visas came through two days before Pesach, we left at once.

We landed in Vienna at 11 a.m., seven hours before the seder was to begin. We'd called ahead from Moscow to our son in Israel, and he had contacted Jewish Agency friends working in Vienna so we could spend the seder with them. Therefore we weren't surprised when a young Israeli stopped the bus between the plane and the airport buildings, climbed on and called out: "Kochubievskys!"

We raised our hands. "Quick!" he said. "Get off the bus" Bewildered, we followed him. We weren't afraid; after all, this wasn't Soviet Russia. But we had no idea what was happening. He bundled us into a small car, gunned the engine and then turned to us, saying: "There's an El Al plane leaving for Israel now. It's on the runway waiting for you." Our son was waiting for us at Ben Gurion Airport with his children, the grandchildren we'd never seen before. It was just three hours before Pesach was to be begin and, still in the coats and boots we'd worn in the snows of Moscow that morning, we raced through the Israeli spring to our son's home. As we sat down to the seder that evening — only the second Pesach seder of our lives — we truly felt we had just been liberated from bondage.

Next Year in Bnai Brak

■ *Adina Raveh, Tel Aviv*

I was 21 when I left the Soviet Union with my parents and my two brothers. It was our parents who had struggled for permission for us all to go. I hadn't been involved in what they were doing. Our first seder in Israel helped me focus on the enormous change that had taken place in our lives.

We spent seder night at the home of my uncle in **Bnai Brak**. I'd attended seders ever since I was a little girl, but this was very different from anything I'd known. There was no longer any sense of keeping what we did secret from the *goyim*. Instead of chanting seder songs quietly as we had in Russia, we sat around the table singing at the tops of our voices. The matza we used came from the corner store, where we could buy as many as we liked. In Russia, our matza had been sent in by Jews in

Switzerland, and we could never be sure they would arrive. The herbs, the egg and the shankbone on the seder dish all came from the local supermarket — rather than from the risky and expensive Ukrainian black market.

When we got to the words "Next year in Jerusalem" things clarified in my mind. "Next year" had finally come. We were free.

The Last Ethiopian Seder, 1991
A Night of Terror and Expectation Before the Exodus

■ *based on an eyewitness report by Micha Odenheimer, journalist and director of a program for Ethiopian olim*

"I brought you to Me on eagles' wings"
— GOD TO ISRAEL, EXODUS 19:4

On Friday night, May 24, 1991, fourteen thousand four hundred Jews from Beita Yisrael crowded into the Israeli Embassy compound in Addis Ababa, the capital. They were caught between a nightmare and a dream, the danger of slaughter by the rebel army that encircled the capital and the opportunity to make aliyah to Israel at the last possible moment before the invasion by the rebels.

Months earlier the Jews of Ethiopia who had lived for centuries as farmers in the Gondar region abandoned their homes, sold their property and migrated often by foot 700 km south to the slums of the capital of the Marxist regime, hoping to leave from there to Israel. Eight weeks earlier the priests (called *kesim*) celebrated at the Israeli Embassy their last Passover in Ethiopia. After purifying themselves in water they laid their hands on ten one-year-old sheep, blessed them, and then ritually slaughtered and roasted them. When the kesim honored me by offering me — an Ashkenazi Orthodox Jew — a piece of the lamb, I hesitated for a moment because their kashrut is different than my own. Yet I knew that eating the Pesach lamb has always been the symbol of inclusion in the Jewish community, so I expressed my solidarity with their Exodus and ate my first Paschal sacrifice.

Only weeks after Pesach the second great Exodus of Beita Yisrael was approaching. The first Exodus was called **Operation**

Moses. In 1984-1985 thousands of starving refugees from war-torn Ethiopia wandered by foot across the desert lands to Sudan. Among them were what Ethiopian Christians call *Falashas* — "intruders," or better *Beita Yisrael* in the language of the Jews (who use the ancient Semitic language of *Gez* as their language of study and prayer). Thousands of Jews perished in this desert trek to freedom, but eventually 6,758 of those who reached Moslem Sudan, were airlifted to Europe and then to Israel in a covert operation organized by the U.S. and Israel.

Now on May 24, 1991, the final Exodus began under the title Operation Solomon. The title reflects the Ethiopian Christian tradition that their monarchy is directly descended from the liaison between the Queen of Sheba (Ethiopia) and King Solomon. (The Lion of Judah is a royal symbol in Ethiopia borne even by their late king Haile Selassie, who was deposed in 1974. He maintained strong diplomatic ties with Jerusalem where he lived in exile in the 1930's during the Italian occupation of Ethiopia).

In 1991 the Marxists who ruled the capital made a deal with Israel for a $35,000,000 bribe (paid by Jewish philanthropists) to release the Jews in a massive airlift just days before the Government lost control of the country.

At the Israeli embassy 14,400 Jews spent all night long in darkness and exceptional calm and discipline. They experienced a mixture of fear and hope (reminiscent of the children of Israel in Egypt on the first seder night). That night the Ethiopian Jews passed from one station to another at the embassy grounds. First the head of the household's identity card was checked and his children counted off and given a sticker with the number of their bus to wear on their forehead. Then all their local money had to be thrown into a box, as demanded by the Ethopian government. Afterwards all their possessions were relinquished, for the Israeli authorities were worried both about bombs and about the lack of space in the planes. Only what they wore — their nicest clothes and gold jewelry — came with them on the planes along with bread which was wrapped in their flowing garments.

I remembered the Biblical verses describing a similar "Night of Vigil" in which no one slept, on Passover evening in Egypt: *"The people took their dough before it was leavened ... wrapped in their cloaks upon their shoulders. The children of Israel borrowed from the Egyptians objects of silver and gold and clothing ... that was ... a Night of Vigil ...."* (EXODUS 12) Even the numbered stickers on the foreheads reminded me of the command, *"This shall serve you as*

a sign upon your hand and as a reminder on your forehead ... that the Lord freed you from Egypt with a mighty hand." (EXODUS 13:9)

Everyone boarded the buses. Arriving at the airport they climbed on to airplanes for the first time in their lives. In less than 24 hours El Al passenger planes as well as Israeli airforce Hercules transports took 14,400 people in the largest, longest, and fastest airlift of refugees in the history of the world; 40 journeys over 1,560 miles and back in 24 hours. As the last plane was loading at 12 p.m. on Shabbat morning, three women arrived on their own at the airport, without papers, surrounded by their children, and pleaded to be allowed to go to Jerusalem before the rebel armies arrive. While the Jewish Agency official tried to turn them away, their tears affected the assistant General Chief of Staff of the Israeli Army Amnon Shahak. He interceded and they were the last ones to join the Exodus from Ethiopia, 1991.

The Legendary Seder in Katmandu

■ *Joel A. Zack*

Flying into Katmandu is a little like arriving in heaven with a window seat. The capital of the tiny Hindu kingdom of Nepal is in the center of a large valley nestled in the Himalayas. Mountains and clouds envelop the city of 300,000.

I arrived in March 1991 after spending two months traveling in India. I had quit my job as an architect in New York to travel around the world, a journey I had fantasized about for as long as I could remember.

The biggest surprise of Katmandu was the huge number of Israeli travelers. There were hundreds of Israelis: invariably young, tough, budget-minded and not particularly religious. Traveling in Southeast Asia after military service has become a common rite of passage for Israelis. Since Nepal has always had good relations with Israel, Israelis are welcome.

I had not been in Katmandu long before I struck up a friendship with a few Israelis. One of them asked me, "Are you going to seder?" Knowing well that Passover must be sometime soon, but that the closest Jewish community was in Calcutta (a few hundred miles away, across some rather formidable mountains), I laughed at the question.

It was then I first learned of the famed "Seder of Katmandu" — a legend of its own. Every Passover for years, three Lubavitcher

Chasidim from Brooklyn fly to Nepal to conduct a seder on the first night of Passover. Hosted at the Israeli embassy, this event is well-known among Israeli travelers. All those traveling in Asia who can possibly arrange it schedule their itineraries so as to be in Katmandu for Erev Pesach. Upon finding the sign-up list, I was astounded to see that I was already guest number 384 — and there were still four days before Passover.

Two days later, the Lubavitchers flew in from Brooklyn, bringing with them matzah and all the requirements for a strictly kosher seder, including more than a few chickens. (Nepalese are strict vegetarians and, in fact, refer to outsiders somewhat derogatorily as "meat-eaters.")

The owners of Pumpernick's Bakery let their business be virtually taken over, and it was transformed into a factory. The kitchen had been kashered and dozens of volunteers washed, chopped and mixed for the seder. Charoset had to be prepared, vegetables cleaned and, of course, how could a seder be complete without chicken soup?

A table was set up to collect the $4 fee. Upon payment, one received a Haggadah, which was to be used as an entry "ticket."

In the two days preceding Passover, one could feel the excitement. There were, it seemed, more Israelis than ever wandering the streets of Katmandu. One saw young people carrying their Haggadot through the narrow streets. Every conversation between Jews of any nationality sooner or later led to the same subject.

Soon enough it was Erev Pesach. I changed into my best clothes (after two months in India, this meant those with the least holes and stains) and my new trekking boots — not yet properly broken in. I then walked a pleasant 30 minutes to the Israeli embassy.

On the grounds of the embassy there was a huge tent, filled with rows of folding chairs. There was seating for 800. I realized this was not going to resemble any seder I had ever attended. I was about to take part in what may have been one of the largest seders anywhere, here on the rooftop of the world.

The seats were already mostly full and people were greeting one another with laughter and tears: old friends from the kibbutz, the moshav, army, high school; friends who had no idea the other had left Tel Aviv; friends and distant relatives who hadn't seen one another in years. In Israel, a country of 5 million, everyone, it seems, is somehow connected.

While the majority of guests were young Israelis, there were also a number of Jews from the United States and Canada.

As sundown approached, the three Chasidim came to the front and led the crowd in songs to celebrate the arrival of the holiday. All three were very young and clearly excited to be there. Their enthusiasm as well as their swaying melodies were contagious, as the crowd became wrapped up in the spiritual nature of the evening.

The wife of the ambassador lit the candles and recited the blessing. The seder was conducted in Hebrew, interrupted frequently for an explanation, story or joke. There were diversions to discuss rabbinic interpretations, to pose questions and to reflect on the meaning of freedom in the direct aftermath of the Persian Gulf war.

While the quality of the cooking did not live up to that of the 800 mothers and grandmothers to which it was undoubtedly being compared, it was warm and tasty. There was no shortage of sweet wine, made in Israel and brought to Nepal via Brooklyn. There was no shortage of matza, either. There was a special plate of matza blessed by the Lubavitcher rebbe broken up and passed among the crowd.

After dinner, the afikoman was found, and as the seder was drawing to its conclusion, someone from the crowd led everyone in singing "Hatikvah."

As I traveled through Asia for the next six months, I would meet many Israelis. They invariably would ask me if I was at the seder. I would answer, "of course."

My Parents' Personal Passover Ritual

■ *Danny Siegel, Jewish poet*
and founder of ZIV, a creative tzedakah fund

Passover in my father's household has always been a celebration of freedom and equality. Two nights a year, twenty to thirty people would sit around our table and join my father in the recitation of the tale of the Jews leaving their bondage in the Land of Egypt.

From the first seder nights I can recall, our guests were our closest friends, plus soldiers (there was World War II and Korea, and they were far away from home), and students at universities in the area who could not afford to go back to Missouri or Illinois or California for the holiday… and a special element: a month before the onset of Passover, my mother would call local institutions for brain-damaged children. She would ask to come down to acquaint herself with six or seven of the children, to talk with them, to bring them things, and to tell them Passover was coming. And then, the afternoon before the first seder, my brother and sister and I would set the tables as my parents took both cars to the institutions, to bring the children back in preparation for the evening in our home.

Besides the regular guests, there were always some new faces — a rotation of doctors, a new patient of my father's who had not seen a seder ritual in years, perhaps the parents of a child my father had delivered in their home long ago. My grandfather was there, of course, and my grandmother, until she died while I was still a teenager, an aunt and some cousins, a friend or two of mine, and the six or seven children.

You will say their noises disturbed the recitations. That is true.

You will say my mother was burdened enough cleaning house and cooking the week through for 50 or 60 people. That is true.

You will say the children needed watching every minute: they would spill things, they would throw up, they might start to shout, and that, too, is true.

But next to each member of my family and in between other couples was one of these children, and each of us was charged with caring for the child, watching over all of them and treating them as best as Moses might have treated them among the masses being taken from Pharaoh's slavery — for we must assume that there were palsied and polioed children three or four thousand years ago, too. Each of us was to bring the message, however dimly perceived, to these children.

And when it came time to eat the meal itself, my father would rise in his white robe, having tasted of the food as prescribed by Jewish law, and would go from seat to seat, cutting the lamb or roast beef and spoonfeeding whoever needed to be fed in such fashion, and joking with each.

The meals would last long past midnight. The mishaps were many, and the fulfillment of the dictum "Any who are hungry shall come in to eat" went slowly, for each had his or her own needs and peculiarities. Yet each was to be fed with utmost care.

In our household on Passover nights, everyone felt at home, everyone was comfortable. No one winced, no one sat in silence while my parents' personal ritual was performed, no one ignored or paid extra attention to what was taking place. Our guests-of-many-years knew what was to happen, and the newcomers soon learned, became momentarily uneasy, then leaned back against their pillows (as free men must have pillows on Passover night), and partook of the wonders of freedom.

(The following afternoons each disease was explained to me. The names were impressive in their Latin and Greek configurations, but the symptoms and the sufferings were a terror to conceive, a travesty of creation. Nevertheless, at our table they were an integral part of our People, of our Greater Family, no more or less normal for their chromosomal defects and their birth traumas, the disorders of their nervous systems and their Down's Syndrome features, than my parents who fed them.)

Those nights, the feeding done, the thanks recited, the singing would begin. It was a dissonant chorus resembling in my early imagination the choir of Heavenly Host, but with flesh and blood instead of halos, twisted words and sounds of human beings in place of the perfect harmonies of angels who need neither food nor drink, nor the affection of my father and my mother.

That is why it is better to be a human being than an angel.

A Seder Activity
Sharing Family Memories

■ *Rabbi Mark B. Greenspan, Beth El Temple, Harrisburg, PA*

My father, Daniel Greenspan, passed away on the third day of Passover, twenty-eight years ago. Though I was only eleven years old at the time, that day had a profound influence on me and has directed my life ever since. I remember the last seder just prior to my father's death as it were yesterday.

All of us have special Passover memories that we cherish. Those memories are a source of strength and wisdom. They challenge us to grow and to perpetuate the values and ideals upon which Passover is founded.

As you celebrate Passover this year, why not devote a few moments to those personal memories, sharing the past with our children.

⮞ Chapter 9
The Four Children

Examining A Midrash: The Biblical and the Rabbinic Four Children

What Is Midrash?

Midrash is a classical Rabbinic method of exploring a Biblical text both to explain internal difficulties in the text and to "search out" (*midrash*) meaning relevant to their own religious and cultural life. It combines careful study of the text along with creative explanations which go well beyond what the historic text says so that the text is made to confront the contemporary situation. The midrash of the Four Children provides an excellent example of such creativity.

We begin with a careful look at the Biblical text itself as if approaching it for the first time in our lives. Then we will compare the Haggadah's Four Children both to the biblical Four Children and to an alternative midrash on the Four Children created by Rabbi Chiya from the same historical period as the one in the Haggadah. (*See the texts on the next two pages.*)

"The Four Children" in the Torah

The "four" children of the midrash derive from four places in the Torah that record some sort of verbatim conversation between parent and child in which the Exodus is mentioned. Interestingly, in only one of these four places does the child ask a question directly pertaining to the Pesach ritual. As one examines these texts the following questions arise:

• What seems to be the event which prompts the child's question?

• What does the child really want to know? (Information? Something else?)

• How would you characterize the educational approach of the parent in answering the question?

• Assuming for a moment the Rabbinic categorization into "four children:" To which child does each passage seem appropriate? Is the identification straightforward, ambiguous, or forced?

"The Four Children" in the Haggadah

The Rabbinic midrash rearranges and recontextualizes the original Biblical texts. After realizing what is new in the midrash, we can then try to determine what was the textual or ideological basis for the innovative interpretation.

We may take the dialogue of the "wise child" in the Haggadah as an example. Amazingly we note that the Rabbis here deleted the Torah's answer to the question (DEUTERONOMY 6:20) and substituted their own: "Tell him about the laws of Pesach — right up to 'we don't proceed to the Afikoman after the Pesach.'" The different answer reveals a different understanding of the question. From the Torah it is clear that the child is asking about the general basis of all the commandments — Why do we perform them? What are they for? The Rabbis, however, understand it as a request for information about the detailed laws of Pesach. Whose answer seems more appropriate to the wise child of today?

Rabbi Chiya's Four Children

The version of the "Four Children" found in the Haggadah dates from the second century C.E. But the Jerusalem Talmud records a version given by Rabbi Chiya. Let's compare them. The answers given to the wise and the simple child have been switched! To the simple child, called here "the stupid one," — we explain the laws of Pesach; to the wise one, the story of the Exodus. Which is the subject matter appropriate for the wise elite — law or history?

The "wicked" child is described more vividly. What bugs him is "all the trouble and bother you put us through every year" in preparing for Pesach and enacting the Seder. It's all a burden to him — "who needs it?" The expression of the parent in addressing the child as "that person" is also interesting. It reflects the distant tone and attitude taken towards the wicked child.

9

The Torah

Deuteronomy 6:20-24

When your child asks you tomorrow: "What is our obligation to these testimonies, laws and regulations that the Lord our God has commanded you?"

Then you are to say to your child: We were slaves to Pharaoh in Egypt, and the LORD took us out of Egypt with a strong hand;

The LORD placed signs and wonders, great and evil ones, on Egypt, on Pharaoh and all his house, before our eyes.

And God took us out of there in order to bring us, to give us the land that God swore to our ancestors;

So the LORD has commanded us to observe all these laws, to hold the LORD our God in awe, for our own good all the days to come, to keep us alive as we are this day.

Exodus 12:22-27

Take a hyssop, dip it in the blood (of the Pesach lamb) in the basin and touch the lintel cord and the two door posts ...
When God sees the blood, the LORD will pass over the entrance ... You are to keep this commandment as a law for you and your children forever.

Now it will be, when you come to the land which the LORD will give you, as promised, you are to keep this rite.

see first column of next page

The Haggadah's Four Children

The Torah alludes in various places to four types of children: one wise, one wicked, one simple, and one who does not know how to ask.

What does the wise child say?

"What are the testimonies, the statutes, and the laws which the Lord your God has commanded you." (DEUTERONOMY 6:20)

"You too must tell him some of the laws of Pesach, up to (THE MISHNA):

"We do not proceed to any 'afikoman' (dessert or after dinner celebrations) after eating the Paschal lamb." (TRACTATE PESACHIM X)

What does the wicked child say?

"Whatever does this service mean to you?" (EXODUS 12:26)

Emphasizing "you" and not himself! And since he excludes himself from the community and rejects a major principle of faith, you should also "set his teeth on edge" and say to

see second column of next page

Rabbi Chiya's Other Four Children
(JERUSALEM TALMUD PESACHIM 10:4)

The Torah alludes (in various places) to four types of children: the wise child, the wicked child, the stupid child, the child who does not know how to ask.

What does the wise child say?

"What are the testimonies, the statutes, and the laws which the Lord your God has commanded us?" (DEUTERONOMY 6:20)

And you shall say to him:

"By a mighty hand the Lord brought us out of Egypt, out of the house of bondage." (EXODUS 13:14)

What does the wicked child say?

"Whatever does this service (or work) mean to you?" (EXODUS 12:26)
What is this drudgery that you bother us with year in and year out?

Since he excludes himself from the community, similarly you

see third column of next page

The Torah	The Haggadah's Four Children	Rabbi Chiya's Other Four Children
(continued)	*(continued)*	*(continued)*
And when your children say to you: "<u>What does this ritual mean to you?</u>" Then say: It is the Passover sacrifice to the LORD, who passed over the houses of the Children of Israel in Egypt, when God struck Egypt and our houses were rescued.	him: "It is because of that which the Lord did for me when I went free from Egypt." (EXODUS 13:8) "Me" and not him! Had he been there, he would not have been redeemed.	should say to him (or regarding him), "It is because of what the Lord did for me." (EXODUS 13:8) For "me" He did it, for "that person" (pointing to the wicked child) He did not do it. If "that person" had been in Egypt, he would never have been worthy of being redeemed, not ever.

The Torah

Exodus 13: 11-14

It shall be when the Lord brings you to the land of the Canaanites, as God promised to you and your ancestors and gave it to you.

Then you are to transfer every first born of the womb to the LORD . . . and every first born of men, among your sons, you are to redeem.

It shall be when your child asks you tomorrow: "<u>What does this mean?</u>"

You are to say: By a strong hand the LORD brought us out of Egypt, out of a house of bondage.

The Haggadah's Four Children

What does the simple child ask?

"What is this?" (EXODUS 13:14)

And you shall say to him:

"By a mighty hand the Lord brought us out of Egypt, out of the house of bondage." (EXODUS 13:14)

Rabbi Chiya's Other Four Children

What does the stupid child ask?

"What is this?" (EXODUS 13:14)

You must teach him the laws of Pesach, that "We do *not* proceed to *afikoman* (dessert or after dinner celebrations) after eating the Paschal lamb." (TRACTATE PESACHIM X) That means he should not leave one group of Pesach celebrants and join another.

In other words, in the Temple era the Paschal lamb was to be eaten only in pre-arranged groups, and the child must not run from one group to another.

The Torah

Exodus 13: 7-9

Matzot are to be eaten for seven days . . .
And you are to tell your child that day, saying:

"It is because of what the LORD did for me, when I went out of Egypt."

It shall be for the sign on your hand and for a reminder between your eyes, in order that the LORD's law may be in your mouth, that by a strong hand did the LORD bring you out of Egypt.

The Haggadah's Four Children

As for the child who does not know how to ask, you should prompt him, as it is said: And you shall tell your son on that day, saying: "It is because of that which the Lord did for me when I went free from Egypt." (EXODUS 13:8)

Rabbi Chiya's Other Four Children

As for the child who does not know how to ask, you should prompt him, first.

9

A Multi-Generational Symposium on the Rabbis' Four Types of Children

Introduction

The Rabbis' famous midrash on the four children serves as a kind of diagnostic chart for parents and educators. The rabbinic "gang of four" (the wise, the wicked, the simple and the one who does not know how to ask) can offer helpful distinctions between the personalities and learning styles of our children. But it may also lead us to counterproductive stereotyping of our potential students (good/evil; brilliant/stupid). Below we have followed the discussion of types of children and attempts at communicating with them from the Torah through the Rabbis of the Talmud to contemporary thinkers and finally to artists who have "commented" on the four children visually. By reading one or two of these at the seder you may inspire a thorough educational debate among parents and children.

■ "Who is Truly Wise?" (Pirkei Avot 4:1) Competing Commentaries on the Rabbis' Wise Child

חָכָם

What does the wise child say?

> "What are the testimonies, the statutes, and the laws which the Lord your God has commanded you?" (DEUTERONOMY 6:20).

You too must tell him some of the laws of Pesach, up to (the end of the Mishna):

> "We do not proceed to any afikoman (dessert or after dinner celebrations) after eating the Paschal lamb." (TRACTATE PESACHIM X)

Clearly the wise child of the Haggadah is portrayed as a knowledgeable, believing and obedient child who formulates long complex questions, distinguishes multiple categories of laws, and accepts the authority of the God who commanded "us." But let's beware of this stereotyped academic brain child. Is this child truly wise?

■ *Don Isaac Abravanel, "The Smart Alec"

This "wise-ass" child is arrogant in his "wisdom." He shows off the distinctions he can make between types of mitzvot. "But you teach him the subtleties of the laws of Pesach down to the last detail in the Mishna." Let the smart alec who appears wise in his own eyes see that there is still much for him to learn. There is double as much wisdom in these laws as in his question. Let the wise grow in wisdom and in humility.

■ **Israel Eldad, "To Know When to Ask"

No! The wise child does not derive his title from his pretense to know-it-all. One who thinks he possesses wisdom already, does not ask at all. "One who does not even know how to ask" has a negative trait typical of the know-it-all. The truly wise child asks, not cynically and mockingly like the rebellious son and not superficially like the simple son. He seeks the essence of things, "What is the true nature of the laws, testimonies and statutes that God has commanded us?"

** **Don Isaac Abravanel** (1437-1508), a Renaissance statesman, philosopher and rabbi who served Ferdinand and Isabella of Spain as a finance minister until his expulsion in 1492. He wrote his commentary on the Pesach Haggadah (*Zevach Pesach*) in Naples, Italy.

** **Dr. Israel Eldad** (died 1996), a Zionist ideologue associated with the Lehi (Stern Gang) guerrillas of the 1940's, is a pungent interpreter of traditional sources in the contemporary Israeli context. He edited *Chronicles* — ancient Jewish history cast in a newspaper format. The quote is freely translated from Eldad, "The Victory of the Wise Child," *Hegyonot Chazal*.

■ The Rasha

The very term "rasha" — רָשָׁע — is difficult to translate: "wicked" and "evil" are very harsh, uncompromising terms for a child. "Rebellious," "mischievous," "recalcitrant," "*chutzpadik*," "impolite," "*wilde chaya*," "naughty," "troublesome," "difficult," "problematic" are also possible.

What leads the rabbi who composed this midrash to interpret the question: "What is this service to you?" as a touchstone for a rebellious child? Why did he think excluding the child from the family and setting his teeth on edge were the most appropriate educational response? What alternative interpretations or responses could be proposed? Here is a sampling of commentaries.

■ *Don Isaac Abravanel from Spain*

This child is determined to embarrass us, the parents (in the midst of the seder before all the guests). He implies that the wine and lambchops are only for our culinary pleasure when he says pointedly, "This service is for you" (not a religious act of worship of God).

■ *R. Shimon ben R. Yehuda Chavillo from Mantova*

This child is not asking a question like the others but making a statement as it says in the Torah: *"When your children come to tell you: What is this service to you?"* (EXODUS 12:26) The tone is arrogant and the intent is to ridicule the ceremony. Instead of asking "why," the child asks sarcastically: What is all this service for, this tiresome bothersome Haggadah that ruins the festive atmosphere and postpones the meal?

■ **Rabbi Elijah the Gaon of Vilna*

The Torah recommends that the parent ignore this (chutzpadik) child and exclude him from the discussion. The answer is directed to the rest of the children. "This service is a response to what God did for me when I went out of Egypt. Not for him (pointing at the child)! Had *he* been there, he would *not* have been redeemed!"

***Elijah the Gaon of Vilna** was a great Talmud scholar towards the end of the 18th C. in Lithuania. His students created the first modern Yeshiva. He was the greatest opponent, "Misnaged," of Hasidism.

■ *Rebellious Daughter of the Talmud*

What alienates a child from Judaism? Sometimes it is an edifice complex — the concern for big expensive buildings and high dues as the entry card to organized worship of God. Consider this ancient rebellious daughter.

> "Miriam daughter of Bilga the Cohen abandoned Judaism and then married an officer of the Hellenistic government. [The story goes that] when the Gentiles entered the Temple, she came and knocked on the top of the altar [the way one disciplines a child] and said: 'Wolf, wolf! You destroyed the property of the Jews [eating up their livestock in unnecessary sacrifices] and You did not help them in the time of their need."
> (*T.B. SUKKAH 56B; TOSEFTA IV 28*)

Her critique of the expense of Jewish observance and of God's lack of concern for Jewish poverty may be behind the wicked or alienated child's question — "What is this sacrifice all about? Why must we go to such trouble [and expense] to make Pesach every year?" (*SCHOLAR'S HAGGADAH, P. 274*)

■ *The Hassidic Seer of Lublin (19th C. Poland)*

In my judgment it is better to be a bad person who knows he is bad than a righteous one who knows that he is righteous. Worst of all is to be a wicked person who thinks he is righteous.

(*MENACHEM HACOHEN, HAGGADAH OF HA-AM*)

9

■ What Lies Behind the Fourth Child's Silence: 'The Child Who Does Not Know How To Ask'

שֶׁאֵינוֹ יוֹדֵעַ

The Midrash recommends:

Create an opening for the child. Just as it says in the Torah: "Tell your child on that very day — 'For this, God did for me — when I left Egypt.'" *(EXODUS 13:8)*

Exploring the Eloquent Silence

Nu! This is quite strange. Jewish children who can't even express wonder? How young are these children? Could there be something obstructing their conversation with their parents? With their tradition?

■ *Marc Angel, The Parent of the Silent Child*

Rabbi Shelomo Halevy Alkabets explains that the child does not ask because he is afraid of making a mistake. He does not know how to phrase his question and lacks confidence. Therefore, the parent should try to lead him into a conversation, to encourage him, to strengthen him, to strengthen his confidence. Through the conversation, the child will have the opportunity of expressing himself. This child has understanding and knowledge, and it is the parent's responsibility to help the child express himself. *(RABBI HAYYIM YOSEF DAVID AZULAI, GEULAT OLAM)*

The child who does not even know how to ask lacks imagination and curiosity. The parent has an obligation to tell the story of the miraculous exodus, thereby stimulating the child's imagination. Even such a child can advance intellectually if he is encouraged to ask questions, to find out the meaning of things. *(RABBI YAACOV HOULI, ME'AM LO'EZ)*

---

* **Rabbi Marc Angel**, an American orthodox rabbi of Sephardic origins, is a proponent of Sephardic tradition and its potential contribution to contemporary Judaism. This quote appears in his *Sephardic Haggadah*, pp. 30-31.

** **Vladimir Jabotinsky** is the founder of the Betar Zionist Revisionist movement that gave birth to the nationalist party Herut headed by Menachem Begin. Though an acculturated Russian Jew, he often reinterprets traditional themes in a Zionist mode in his novels and poems. This quote is freely translated from "The Four Sons" reprinted in *Sefer Hamoadim: Pesach* edited by Yom Tov Levinsky, p. 252-253.

*** **Yariv Ben Aharon**, a secular kibbutznik, a novelist and Jewish scholar is involved in the creative appropriation of classical sources within the revolutionary Zionist tradition of the socialist Kibbutz. This question is freely translated from "The Four Children," *In the Kibbutz*.

The four children are paralleled by four kinds of parents. The wise parent encourages the child to learn and to ask. The wicked parent treats religious symbolism with scorn, separating himself from the community. The naive parent does not trouble to study and learn, and has no deep knowledge of Torah and Jewish tradition. In each of these three cases, the children follow the models set by their parents.

The child who does not know how to ask is a most unfortunate child. Children are naturally curious and are always asking questions. To find a child who is unable to ask is shocking, even frightening. Such a child may exist because of the domineering nature of the parent. A parent who is constantly criticizing the child, always silencing him, and frequently showing him disrespect — such a parent deprives the child of self-esteem. The child suppresses questions because he is afraid.

The Haggadah teaches parents to reevaluate their own roles in relationship to their children, to open channels of communication. If parents and children can sit around the same table, can celebrate the festival, can discuss words of Torah — then there is hope. *(RABBI MARC ANGEL, THE SEPHARDIC HAGGADAH)*

■ **Zeev Jabotinsky, In Praise of the Unquestioning Personality**

No! I don't agree with the advice of the Haggadah here. The Haggadah says open him up to critical thinking. In my judgment the parent should be silent. Just kiss this child on the forehead for faithfully maintaining his loyalty to those sanctified traditions. The love of knowledge, the philosophical quest is important but the supreme wisdom is to accept the treasures of the past without second guessing, without evaluating their historical origins and their pragmatic utility. It is essential to cherish and preserve that kind of respectful wisdom and not to tarnish it with unnecessary talk.

■ ***Yariv Ben Aharon, "A Thunderous Silence"***

Open up the child who has not learned to ask. Lead him on the path to becoming a questioning personality, one who inquires about the way of the world. Open him up to formulate his own queries. For without questions your ready-made

9

answers remain inert and there is no common ground between you. The silence of the child can be thunderous. The silence of the one who does not know how to ask may be the result of not having found an appropriate address to express queries. Deeply meaningful silences can issue forth secrets that resound throughout the whole world ... Model for the child the adults who know how to ask of themselves questions. As the rabbis said: "If the child and the spouse are unable to ask, let the parent ask himself." *(T.B. PESACHIM 115A)* Then there is a good chance that the child will learn to ask as well.

■ *Silent Children and their Mothers*

The Midrash of the Four Children recommends that "אַתְּ" — "you" — should open up the child who does not know how to ask. You be the first teacher who helps the child to wonder and to inquire. In Mishnaic Hebrew "אַתְּ" simply means "you" without any gender identification, but the new kibbutz Haggadah understands "אַתְּ" as in Biblical Hebrew as "you feminine:" You, the mother, are the child's first teacher.

Perhaps an alternative reading is possible: "you" as a collective form; the organized Jewish community, have a collective responsibility to teach all the alienated, silent Jews.
(THE SCHOLAR'S HAGGADAH, P. 278)

■ *Rabbi Levi Yitzchak of Berditchev (19th C. Poland) — Job and the Silent One*

Whenever Rabbi Levi Yitzchak of Berditchev came to that passage in the Haggadah which deals with the Four Sons and read in it about the fourth son, he who does not know how to ask, he said:

"The one who knows not how to ask, that is myself, Levi Yitzchak of Berditchev. I do not know how to ask you, Lord of the world, and even if I did know, I could not bear to do it. How could I venture to ask you: Why ... we are driven from one exile into another, why our foes are allowed to torment us so much?

"But in the Haggadah the parent of the one who does not know how to ask is told: 'It is for you to disclose the answer to the child.'

"And the Haggadah refers to the Torah in which it is written, 'And you shall tell your son.' *(EXODUS 13)*

"Lord of the world, am I not your child?" (Even if I cannot formulate the questions, you can begin to answer them for me.)

■ *Four Children, Four Generations and "The Orphan in History"*

One might identify four generations — since the great emigration of Eastern European Jews to the New World began in the 1880's. The *first* generation of the immigrants is the WISE child who knows and feels comfortable with Jewish tradition. The *second* generation is the REBEL who in the name of progress and westernization rejects their parents' Judaism after having imbibed it at home. The *third* generation is assimilated. There is little knowledge and little resentment, but there is still SIMPLE curiosity about the customs of their grandparents.

Finally, a *fourth* generation is without knowledge or even mild acquaintance is born. These DO NOT KNOW HOW TO ASK. They might be called "orphans in history" lacking any of the resources of Jewish wisdom against which to struggle and from which to draw personal meaning.

As a child, growing up on Manhattan's East Side, I lived among Jewish WASP's. My father had changed his name from "Cohen" to "Cowan" when he was 21. So I was brought up to think of myself as a "Cowan" — the Welsh word for stonecutter, not a "Cohen" — a member of the Jewish priesthood. My family celebrated Christmas and always gathered for Easter dinner of ham and sweet potatoes. Though they never converted to Christianity my parents sent me to an Episcopalian prep school with a mandatory chapel service. In those years, I barely knew what a Passover seder was. I didn't know anyone who practiced "archaic" customs such as keeping kosher or lighting candles

9

Friday night. When I fell in love and married Rachel, a New England Protestant whose ancestors came here in the 17th century, it didn't matter in the least that we were formally an interfaith marriage. I had become an orphan without a history.

— *SAUL COHEN OR PAUL COWAN, AN ORPHAN IN HISTORY*

Listen to Paul Cowan: a "fourth generation" Jew who later discovered how to ask and became Jewishly involved. Does his story speak to any of you? Why did the rift develop within the chain of tradition? Can you offer any ports of reentry into Jewish life in which a dialogue between the individual and the resources of the past can begin? Can you imagine what the fifth generation will be like?

■ *The Four Children*

We are always proud, forever
speaking of the wise one, the wise child.
What about the bad one (recalling, of course,
Father Flanagan's "There's no such thing as a bad kid")?
If we have none of those, why are so many rabbis
making rounds in the Big Houses across our fair land?
Who are these ghosts in the minimum,
medium, and maximum prisons? Figments?
(We had our Uncle Simcha who hid out
with Grandpa for a few weeks. I think it was
Prohibition and he was mixed up with some,
shall we say, undesirable fellows.)
Now comes the hard part, the special two —
"simple" and "unable-to-ask."
You may say "simple" means nice or "easygoing,"
the kid who likes everything, is happy, and
makes no demands. It's the one you refer to
now that he or she is grown up when you say,
"Joe (or Nancy) was an easy child." All right, then —
that's three out of four. But that still leaves
"the one who doesn't know how to ask."
I think the pictures in the Haggadah are wrong,
painting children so small.
They shift; they mislead. It doesn't mean:
"so young they can't formulate the words."
It means... We know what it means.
And if we just say it, with the pride of the first,
maybe this year more can come out of their hiding places.

— *Danny Siegel*

ᔕ Chapter 10
A Symposium About Slavery and Freedom
An Anthology of Quotations

"We were slaves to Pharaoh" /
"We are slaves now"

The Haggadah recalls slavery as a historic moment from the past — "we were slaves to Pharaoh in Egypt," but it also declares that "we still are slaves now, though next year we will be free." Are we today still slaves — if not politically and economically, then psychologically or spiritually? That is the theme of the symposium of famous quotes found below.

Directions:

- Reproduce a group of ten quotations for all the participants.

- Ask everyone to choose a quote about freedom and slavery that expresses something felt deeply.

- Ask participants at the table to read the quote they chose and explain their reasons for choosing it.

- Hopefully a discussion will emerge regarding the true nature of freedom.

1 *No human being is free who is not master of himself.*
— EPICTETUS (ANCIENT GREEK PHILOSOPHER)

2 *Freedom is not worth having if it does not connote freedom to err.*
— MAHATMA GANDHI (20TH C. INDIAN FREEDOM "FIGHTER")

3 *Better a thin freedom than a fat slavery.*
— FOLK PROVERB

4 *There is no boredom like that which can afflict people who are free, and nothing else.*
— RALPH BARTON PERRY

5 *A man may not always eat and drink what is good for him; but it is better for him and less ignominious to die of the gout freely than to have a censor officially appointed over his diet, who after all could not render him immortal.*
— GEORGE SANTAYANA (20TH C. EXISTENTIALIST PHILOSOPHER)

6 *Security is never an absolute ... The government of a free people must take certain chances for the sake of maintaining freedom which the government of a police state avoids because it holds freedom to be of no value.*
— A. BARTHOLINI

7 *Praised be You who has not made me a slave.*
— RABBI AHA BEN JACOB (BABYLONIAN TALMUD SCHOLAR)

8 *None are more hopelessly enslaved than those who falsely believe they are free.*
— GOETHE (GERMAN 19TH C. WRITER)

9 *The only freedom which deserves the name is that of pursuing our own good, in our own way, so long as we do not attempt to deprive others of theirs, or impede their efforts to obtain it.*
— J.S. MILL (ENGLISH 19TH C. POLITICAL PHILOSOPHER)

10 *He is the free man whom the truth makes free, and all are slaves beside.*
— COWPER

11 *Slaves are free when they are satisfied with their lot; free persons are really slaves when they seek more than their lot.*
— TACHKIMONI

12 *Freedom is taken, not given.*
— AHAD HAAM (ZIONIST, 20TH C. THINKER)

10

13 *I am for those that have never been master'd!*
For men and women whose tempers have never been master'd,
For those whom laws, theories, conventions, can never master.
— WALT WHITMAN (19TH C. AMERICAN POET): *As I Sat Alone*, 1856

14 *Those who deny freedom to others deserve it not for themselves,*
and, under a just God, cannot long retain it.
— ABRAHAM LINCOLN (U.S. PRESIDENT DURING THE CIVIL WAR), 1859

15 *Better to be a free bird than a captive king.*
— DANISH PROVERB

16 *No human is wholly free. One is a slave to wealth, or to*
fortune, or the laws, or the people restrain him from acting
according to his will alone.
— EURIPIDES (ANCIENT GREEK PLAYWRIGHT)

"No man can command my conscience."
FROM MARTIN LUTHER (16TH C. REFORMATION)
— BEN SHAHN, 1956, THE BIOGRAPHY OF A PAINTING

Licensed by Estate of Ben Shahn. © 1996. Licensed by VAGA, NY, NY.

17 *Who, then, is free? The wise who can command their passions,*
who fear not want, nor death, nor chains, firmly resisting their
appetites and despising the honors of the world, who rely
wholly on themselves, whose angular points of character have
all been rounded off and polished.
— HORACE (ROME, C. 25 B.C.E.)

18 *It is not good to be too free. It is not good to have everything one*
wants.
— BLAISE PASCAL (FRANCE): *PENSEES*, 1670

19 *Since the general civilization of mankind, I believe there are*
more instances of the abridgment of the freedom of the people
by gradual and silent encroachments of those in power than by
violent and sudden usurpations.
— JAMES MADISON (U.S. PRESIDENT), 1788

20 *The Merciful demands that your servant be your equal. You*
should not eat white bread, and he black bread; you should not
drink old wine, and he new wine; you should not sleep on a
featherbed and he on straw. Hence it was said, Whoever
acquires a Hebrew slave acquires a master.
— TALMUD

21 *When is a man free? Not when he is driftwood on the stream*
of life, . . . free of all cares or worries or ambitions . . . He is not
free at all — only drugged, like the lotus eaters in the Odyssey . . .
To be free in action, in struggle, in undiverted and purposeful
achievement, to move forward towards a worthy objective
across a fierce terrain of resistance, to be vital and aglow in the
exercise of a great enterprise — that is to be free, and to know
the joy and exhilaration of true freedom. A man is free only
when he has an errand on earth.
— ABBA HILLEL SILVER (20TH C. REFORM RABBI AND ZIONIST LEADER)

22 *Because I was born a slave, I love liberty more than you.*
— LUDWIG BOERNE (GERMAN JEW), 1832

23 *I hold a jail more roomy than would be the whole world if I*
were to submit to repression.
— SAMUEL GOMPERS (AMERICAN JEW,
FOUNDER OF THE AMERICAN FEDERATION OF LABOR), 1925

24 *Though in themselves trivial ends are not important — indeed*
it is of their essence to be unimportant — they give one a mea-
sure of breathing space. How important it is to the sense of one's
autonomy and worth to have some such area of arbitrary and
trivial concerns reserved to oneself.
— UNKNOWN

25 *Neither heavenly nor earthly, neither mortal nor immortal have we created you, so that you might be free according to your own will and honor, to be your own creator and builder. To you alone we gave growth and development depending on your own free will. You bear in you the germs of a universal life.*

— PICO DELLA MIRANDOLA (ITALIAN RENAISSANCE HUMANIST):
ORATIO DE HOMINIS DIGNITATE

26 *The serious threat to our democracy is not the existence of foreign totalitarian states. It is the existence within our own personal attitudes and within our own institutions of conditions which have given a victory to external authority, discipline, uniformity and dependence upon the "Leader" in foreign countries. The battlefield is also accordingly here — within ourselves and our institutions.*

— JOHN DEWEY (20TH C. AMERICAN PHILOSOPHER OF EDUCATION)

27 *The ambiguous meaning of freedom was to operate throughout modern culture: on the one hand, the growing independence of man from external authorities, on the other hand, his growing isolation and the resulting feeling of individual insignificance and powerlessness. Freedom from the traditional bonds of medieval society, though giving the individual a new feeling of independence, at the same time made him feel alone and isolated, filled him with doubt and anxiety, and drove him into new submission and into a compulsive and irrational activity.*

— ERICH FROMM (20TH C. GERMAN JEWISH PSYCHOLOGIST),
ESCAPE FROM FREEDOM

28 *What then is the meaning of freedom for modern man?*

He has become free from the external bonds that would prevent him from doing and thinking as he sees fit. He would be free to act according to his own will, if he knew what he wanted, thought, and felt. But he does not know. He conforms to anonymous authorities and adopts a self which is not his. The more he does this, the more powerless he feels, the more is he forced to conform. In spite of a veneer of optimism and initiative, modern man is overcome by a profound feeling of powerlessness and enslavement.

— ERICH FROMM, *ESCAPE FROM FREEDOM*

29 *Difference is the condition requisite to all dignity and to all liberation. To be aware of oneself is to be aware of oneself as different. To be is to be different.*

— ALBERT MEMMI (20TH C. NORTH AFRICAN ZIONIST THINKER)

An oppressed person must never expect others to hand him his liberation… The oppressed person must take his destiny in his own hands. My life must no longer depend on any treaty, often signed with other ends in mind, by anyone with anyone… Better still, no one owes us anything….

We should not have had to ask ourselves piteously and in vain, why the Pope was silent, or why the Americans abandoned us, why the Russians didn't budge.

And why not the Red Cross? And the ASPCA!

Liberty is not a gift. Bestowed, conceded, protected by someone else, it is denied and it vanishes.

Our liberation must depend on our own fight for it….

One never really shakes off oppression except by revolt.

— ALBERT MEMMI

30 *Self-negation is slavery.*
Self-affirmation is freedom.
We go to Zion to be ourselves.

— LUDWIG LEWISOHN

10

The first mark of the position of a minority is its complete lack of self-determination. Do what it may, the terms of its very existence are fixed for it by the mere weight and tendencies and habits of the surrounding majority. And this is no less true when that majority is friendly than when it is hostile.

Favor and disfavor are the moods of the masters.

— LUDWIG LEWISOHN

31 *We have continued to celebrate Passover because we have always been in the desert and we have always awaited our liberation.*

— ALBERT MEMMI

32 *When Moses wished to free his people from Egyptian slavery, the Jews were the first to rise against him and threaten to denounce him to the Egyptian authorities.*

— MAX NORDAU (19TH-20TH C. AUSTRIAN INTELLECTUAL AND ZIONIST), 1898

Chapter 11
Elijah's Cup:
A Time for Vengeance or for Reconciliation?

Pour Out Your Wrath on Our Murderous Enemies
שְׁפֹךְ חֲמָתְךָ —

Elijah has come to represent polar visions. Elijah as described in the Book of Kings is a bitter, zealous prophet escaping by the skin of his teeth from Jezebel's and Ahab's systematic execution of prophets and promotion of pagan worship in Israel. Given the situation it is no surprise that he demands that God take vengeance. Yet Elijah as described by the prophet Malachi also comes "to reconcile the divided hearts of parents and children" (including the Divine parent God and His human children). The rabbis described Elijah as a forerunner of the messianic era.

> He will come not to judge and to distinguish good from evil, the pure from the unpure, but to retrieve those who were pushed far away, who had become alienated from their families because of fear and trouble. He comes "to resolve disputes among the rabbis themselves" and "to make peace between Israel and the nations." He is a messenger, not of wrathful justice, but of love and reconciliation of hearts.
>
> (MISHNA EDUYOT 8:7 ACCORDING TO MAIMONIDES, RABAD, AND THE MEIRI)

Medieval Jewish folklore made Elijah into a mysterious and beneficent visitor who appears just when one most needs him with good news, with a bit of money, or simply to be the tenth for a minyan.

We prefer to retain both perspectives of Elijah. On the one hand, if Elijah can heal our pain, and offer us a renewed relationship within our own families, then perhaps the deep need for righteous anger need not inform the vision of the future. On the other hand, if we disregard the existence of radical evil as a potential for the present and the future, then we may impair our view of reality and blind ourselves to ongoing dangers that ought to be met resolutely with eyes open.

The Kibbutz Debates:
To Pour or Not to Pour Out Your Wrath!

The Israeli secular kibbutz has freely amended the traditional Haggadah to reflect their own twentieth century exodus and return to Israel. In different eras they vacillated over the inclusion of *"Pour out your wrath."* In the Haggadah of Kibbutz Ramat HaKovesh, 1943-1944, *"Pour Out Your Wrath"* appears on the front page of the Haggadah, in bold letters, and selections about the Warsaw Ghetto Uprising have been inserted. But in the Haggadah of the Kibbutz Movement (HaMeuchad), 1971, a debate arose among the editors: should *"Pour Out Your Wrath"* be included in the new version for the 1970s? The elders of the movement were consulted. Yitzchak Tabenkin ruled: "No! We are celebrating our national freedom, not cursing nations. We are not giving out grades to allies and to enemies on their behavior. However, if a kibbutz (like the Ghetto Fighters Kibbutz) has members who are Holocaust survivors, then they have every right to express their wrath ... and to curse their persecutors. This is their spiritual vengeance, their memorial to the Holocaust! Therefore, we will make available to those kibbutzim of survivors a page of 'Pour Out Your Wrath' that can be attached to the Kibbutz movement's standard Haggadah that will not otherwise contain it."

Tales of the Red Matza

■ *by Stuart Schoffman* (April 4, 1991, The Jerusalem Report)

In 1991, Nabila Shaalan, a Syrian delegate to the United Nations Human Rights Commission, commended a "very important work that demonstrates unequivocally the historical reality of Zionist racism" — namely a tome penned in 1985 by Mustafa Tlass, Syrian minister of defense, entitled "The Matza of Zion," a justification of the notorious Damascus blood accusation of 1840.

The blood libel made its debut in Norwich, England in 1144, and consists of the bizarre allegation that Jews, in their pre-Passover preparations, slaughter Christians (children preferably) to use their blood in the baking of matza. The solemn prohibition in Judaism against the consumption of blood in any form has never fazed the libelers. The fantasy has mainly to do with the ceremonial re-crucifixion of Jesus. A century later, in 1255, a lad named Hugh of Lincoln was found dead in the Jewish part of town and under torture, a Jew named Copin confessed. Copin and 18 other Jews were hanged without trial, and the event was, later immortalized not only by Chaucer in *The Prioress's Tale*, but in no fewer than 21 folk songs collected in the 1890s in Child's classic compendium *English and Scottish Popular Ballads*. There's a version to be found in an American anthology of Ozark Mountain folk songs as recently as 1973.

On the first day of Pesach, 1475, in Trent, England, a three year old Christian boy named Simon disappeared. The local bishop accused the Jews. Even though the genuine murderer was later discovered, the falsely accused Jews were burned and the rest of the community exiled. In the course of the investigation dead Simon's wounds reportedly began to bleed again miraculously. He was declared a saint and pilgrimages to his grave were common.

A famous Jewish literary rendition of the Golem of Prague legends involving Rabbi Judah Loew, putative 16th-century inventor of the great avenging monster, credits the golem with saving the community by placing at the doorstep of its true killers a Christian corpse planted in the Jewish quarter.

Despite the general opposition of high ecclesiastical authorities, there have been some 200 documented cases of blood accusation, ranging down to the most infamous example of our own century, the Mendel Beilis case in Czarist Russia in 1911 engraved fictionally in Bernard Malamud's *The Fixer*.

The episode revived in Tlass's "Matza of Zion" involves the disappearance of one Capuchin Father Tomaso and his manservant in Damascus on February 5, 1840. A confession was extracted from a Jewish barber. Western Jewry rose to the crisis with a series of emergency measures in England, France and the United States. Many historians credit the Damascus Affair with having galvanized American Jews into an encompassing national community for the first time.

In the early 1970, Saudi King Faisal told a Cairo newsman: "Two years ago when I was in Paris, police discovered the bodies of five children … Afterwards it turned out that Jews killed the children to mix their blood into their bread."

The Spirit of Equality and Reconciliation at the Seder

■ *by Franz Rosenzweig* (20th C. German Jewish philosopher)

The welding of people into a people takes place in its deliverance … Among the many meals of the spiritual year, the evening meal of the Passover at which the father of the household gathers together all his family is the meal of meals. It is the only one that from first to last has the character of worship; hence the Seder ("Order") is, from first to last, liturgically regulated. From the very start the word "freedom" sheds its light upon it.

Freedom expresses itself in the fact that the youngest child is the one to speak, and that what the parent says at the table is adapted to this child's personality and his degree of maturity. In contrast to all instruction, which is necessarily autocratic and never on a basis of equality, the sign of a **true and free social intercourse** is this, that the one who stands — relatively speaking — nearest the periphery of the circle, gives the cue for the level on which the conversation is to be conducted. For this conversation must include him. No one who is there in the flesh shall be excluded in the spirit. The **freedom of a society is always the freedom of everyone who belongs to it**. Thus this meal is a symbol of the people's vocation for freedom. The parent of the family speaks, the household listens, and only in the further course of the evening is there more and more common independence until, in the songs of praise and the table songs of the second part of the meal, songs which float between divine mystery and the jesting mood begot by wine, the **last shred of autocracy in the order of the meal dissolves into community**.

This is the deepest meaning of the farewell which those who participate in the evening meal bid one another: *Next year in Jerusalem!* In every house where the meal is celebrated a cup filled with wine stands ready for the prophet **Elijah**, the precursor of the shoot from the stock of Jesse, who is forever *"turning the hearts of the parents to their children and the hearts of the children to their parents."*

(*THE STAR OF REDEMPTION*, PP. 317-319)

PART III

BACKGROUND ESSAYS

Chapter 12

On Passover and Family Education

■ *essays by Rabbi David Hartman*

The Art of Storytelling

■ *by Rabbi David Hartman*

Jews realized that people needed a text in order to help them along in reliving the story. The Haggadah is not a prayer book or revelation of the word of God in which every word has to be uttered in its prescribed place. It is not like daven-ing (praying the set prayers). A tragedy of the Pesach Seder is that it often became like davening. A service to zoom through. Rather, it is meant to be a play in which people act very important roles.

Notice that a major concern of Pesach night is about how to tell the story. Indeed, much of the ritual takes place in order to keep the kids up and awake. *(CF. PESACHIM 109A)* That expresses the urgency of getting the story across. Jews used to throw around the matza. They used to dip foods so the kids would say, "What are you doing that for?" "Why am I dipping the food?" — and the parent responded, "Wait until later." It created suspense.

Now for those children who go to Hebrew school, the teacher makes them repeat four thousand times, *"Mah-nishtanah ha-lailah ha-zeh ...."* By the time of the night of Pesach, they say, "Now what do I get for it? It was all over so fast." There was no drama, no surprise. Nothing is going to happen that night that was not expected. That is how the experience is killed, because the parent has not been trained to be a dramatic story teller. Passover frees the Jew to allow his imagination full rein.

The Haggadah also mentions the five rabbis in the town of Bnei Brak who used to spend the whole night talking about Passover. They are trying to tell us, "Don't be imprisoned by the text. People should interpret. The text is only a minimum. Talk. Discuss. You are free. Don't let the printed word paralyze the imagination. Let the typed page be only that which fertilizes the imagination, and does not enchain it."

The educators of the Talmud try to bring this home by speaking about four sons: the wise, the wicked, the simple, and the one who did not know how to ask a question. The parent has to learn not to pontificate one identical rendition to every child in the family, because not everyone in the family hears the same way. Each one has to receive a different answer.

The family as a unit of community does not demand herd conformity, but it requires listening to the intangible uniqueness of each member. The task of the family is not to preach one message but rather to allow the integral human being to find himself in the family context. Individuality and family consciousness are not antithetical; the liberated person can be present in the context of the wholeness of community. The Jew has to learn to speak to each member of the family according to his/her singularity.

The parent nourishes individuality in the family, being challenged to look at each child differently. The Haggadah speaks about four children. They could speak about eighty children. Thus on one level, the night of Pesach creates peoplehood, illuminating the drama of history, painting with large strokes the epic of liberation which pitted prophet against king. Yet the Seder focuses on how to speak to different children and to listen to their questions. Different queries are born which express the singularity and uniqueness of individual people in the family. Jews nourish the unique in a festival that celebrates the nation. The "I" and the "we" are not antithetical dimensions.

This is the difficulty in leading a seder: The leader has to affirm the singularity of individuals even while leading family participation in a commonality. How are collectivity and uniqueness created? How does one build individuality within the framework of being part of a historical drama. How does one fashion rootedness in people without abandoning each person's identity. How can each human being find his/her uniqueness in a matrix of family and of community. These are the dramatic challenges. I would not pretend that Jews always succeed. The function of the holiday and its ritual is to point to what could be. Never is it wholly achieved. Pesach comes each year so we can try again.

In my own perception, the symbols of Pesach center around the role of the family which mediates a sense of history. Pesach does not merely celebrate social ethics, or universal human freedom. It is not an ethical get-together, nor a protest sit-in. Passover features in fact the link between the dignity of the lone human being and the importance of peoplehood and nationhood — the family, which is central in the recital of the Passover story.

The family introduces relational consciousness; it mirrors a person's identity as a relational being, in place of a self-sufficient unit. The family furthermore grounds the notion of life as a gift, and concretizes the fact that I am because others are. To live within a family is to learn to receive gifts from one's progenitors.

I am because something happened before me. Family consciousness trains the ability to be a creature, to receive, and not to live with the illusion of self-sufficiency. The degree to which a child can accept parents is the degree to which one can accept dependency as a permanent feature of existence.

By "dependency" I mean an awareness that striving or pretending to be absolutely self-sufficient is idolatry. A person's acceptance of finitude and of humanity involves understanding that one exists because something else outside of oneself was and is. Living with that awareness; the recognition of relationship; a relational consciousness, constitutes our point of departure.

It is not true that I first am an "I"; that I put my "I" together; and that then after I put my "I" together, I go to others. This is a myth. There is no "I" which is complete alone. A person puts himself together only if he puts himself in the context of relationship. The primary point of consciousness is relationship. "It is not good for man to be alone" *(Genesis 2:18)* is not merely a functional category; but rather, it is an ontological category. The human is not complete alone. Consciousness is relational. The family mediates the world, but the individual is not swallowed by the family and its past. The freedom of choice cannot begin before one receives something from one's parents.

I have no difficulty accepting my parents because I have no difficulty recognizing that I am because two people decided one day to make love to each other. And when people ask, "How did you choose your Jewish identity. Did you first try being a Buddhist or a Hindu, or . . . ?" I reply, "I have no difficulty receiving gifts. My Jewishness is a gift; my parents gave it to me." An important issue is, "Which gifts do you take and make part of your own convictions?" One can also throw away gifts. — But I have no difficulty receiving gifts. In fact, I am very grateful to my lifelong friend because he happened to know a girl with whom I went on a blind date — and we fell in love and this has changed my life for thirty years already. I do not mind receiving things from people. But to live totally out of my lonely ego without external resources would be truly impossible.

Crucial here is that one's sense of history begins in this family context. The father and mother are story tellers. The parent brings me into contact with my historical roots, with my grandfather and a world other than me. Whether it is relevant, the child will decide; but the parent must witness to a history and a memory that is needed in order to realize that there is a dimen-

12

sion to existence beyond the self. Jews who learn to honor their parents escape narcissism and acquire a memory. The past need not predetermine the future but let the children know that the present is open to a wide-ranging drama that preceded them. The parents are the feeders of history.

Parents should not determine their children's future, but they must open for them their past. The Haggadah of the night of Pesach transforms the parents into storytellers. It is a very serious task to tell stories.

The Covenant of Common Destiny: The Leap of Solidarity

■ *by Rabbi David Hartman*

On Passover Jews say, "We were slaves." We were objects exploited by Pharaoh; and there is talk about a common suffering, a shared pain. We had no Law, no Torah in the first Passover; there was only a common suffering. Joseph Soloveitchik called that kind of suffering "*brit goral,*" the **covenant of destiny**. This constitutes a bold statement concerning what Passover may mean.

Some might imagine faith to mean an inner transformation; a leap into God. Judaism, however, does not begin with a leap of faith, nor even with a leap of commitment to mitzvah. Rather than with a spiritual transformation of personal identity, Judaism commences with a leap of solidarity, an unmediated empathy with our history.

I cannot emphasize too much how essential this is in order to clarify so much of Western civilization's misunderstanding of Judaism. Judaism begins with an identification with a singular community that has a particular history. It is to say, "I am prepared to go into Egypt and suffer with this people." It is the free and lordly prince Moses saying to slaves, "You are my brothers." It is lining up with the Jews. Whether the line is in Buchenwald, or Egypt, or any other place in history; it is saying, "Your destiny is mine. I share whatever life will give to you. It is my reality. I see no way of being safe if you are threatened." Rejecting the option of trying to save one's own life, Esther came forward. Revealing his Jewish identity to the Egyptians and his family, Joseph remembered his brothers and reentered their lives. The Moses story, the Esther story, and the Joseph story present

individuals who in some way might have been safe alone, but who for some mysterious reason make this choice to be visible as a Jew. "Your history is my history," they tell their family.

What does this have to do with religion? If religion is doctrine, Judaism is not a religion. Jews, without knowing precisely how to define themselves, are a people saying, "For some reason, I cannot be other than with this *mishpacha* (family). Why, I don't know. It is not a family defined by blood; I become part of this people through choice. I share what history and life will give, feeling that there is no option to be outside their struggles."

The sense of being claimed by this people's history is reflected in Maimonides' claim that one who fulfills all the mitzvot but does not share in Israel's joys and sufferings has no share in immortality. *(CF. MISHNEH TORAH, HILKHOT TESHUVAH III 11)* **Peoplehood is our cathedral.** This is the strange category that makes Jews lonely in Western civilization. We look tribal. We look ethnic. But it is not just that: rather, peoplehood mediates the living God of Israel. One has to be in Egypt first before one can stand at Sinai. Judaism begins neither with the Ten Commandments, nor with a pledge of faith. Rather than with the covenantal experience at Sinai, Judaism begins with the story of slaves in Egypt. I was a slave and God brought me out. I was there. Unless that suffering is my suffering, I have not begun to understand Judaism. That is why a Jew must eat the maror, the bitter herb. It symbolizes this pain of mine.

This is the mystical experience in Judaism. The Jew becomes a mystic not by becoming one with God, but by absorbing the historical drama of this community. **We leap into peoplehood.** This was the most difficult thing to teach to people who came to me to convert to Judaism. To expound about God, Torah, mitzvah, was easy, but the challenge was to help them understand that they have to be like Ruth. "Wherever the Jews go, you go. You are not free. You're totally claimed by Israel's history. I am claimed by these people's dream. I feel I must keep these dreams alive."

My grandparent has to live in what I do. Perhaps this explicates the deep meaning of the resurrection of the dead. I have to fashion a society where my grandparents' dreams have a place. It is not enough to build Israel on the basis of my own dreams. I have to construct in the light of all my zeda's and bubbie's dreams.

The God of Surprise: "Next Year in Jerusalem"

■ by Rabbi David Hartman

Central to the Exodus story and the Pesach seder is the recounting of the ten plagues. As moderns educated in natural science, on the lawful order of the world, the story strikes us as childish, as primitive, as mythological. Yet we may be missing the point of these extraordinary events if we understand it as ancient superstition. Instead the miracle is a symbol of spontaneity in history, a faith in the changeability of oppressive regimes. What appears as fate, the necessity of a small people subject to an invulnerable empire is revealed as an illusion. The language of the supernatural miracle is the Bible's way of undermining the acquiescence of humans to the "way things have to be," to the political "facts of nature" created by powerful dictators.

There is an unpredictable Power present in the universe.

A people arising from helplessness, utter destruction, and complete impoverishment, the movement from Egypt to the desert, was a radical leap. It was not a steady process; not a gradual development. The plagues and the crossing of the Red Sea signalled the breaking in of Power that confronted tyrannical hegemonies which refused to accept ultimate divine Sovereignty.

Belief in miracle is the basis of the "hope model" of Judaism. **Exodus becomes a call to revolutionary hope regardless of the conditions of history.** The act of protest against their environment can occur because the Jews possess a memory bank that structures what they think is possible. The Exodus becomes vital because it tells people that they are able to hope. The order that people observe in the cosmos is not irreversible. **Tomorrow will not necessarily be like today.**

Belief in the doctrine of creation reinforces the belief in miracle. Creation means that the world that came about at a certain moment could be recreated in a new constellation if God so wills it. Spontaneity and surprise characterize divinity. Not everything is a recurring pattern. The cosmos is not a Nietzschean wheel of eternal recurrence. **Creation and the miracles of Exodus protest against the despair of the book of Ecclesiastes.** The Preacher of Ecclesiastes proclaims that the world is '*hevel*' [vanity]. Nothing really changes; all is endless repetition. A generation comes, a generation goes. A child dies, a wife, a father…all is in vain, without significance.

The Exodus provided the memory that made hope a very real possibility. *Being* is not inalterable. *Becoming* marks a human being's ontology. Radical surprise becomes an important feature. New possibilities are always present; history can change.

Fundamental to this whole posture, then, is the belief in "*Le-shana ha-ba-a b'Yerushalayim*" ("Next year in Jerusalem!"). The key term is "*ha-ba-a*," future; next year. Tomorrow can be other than yesterday.

Life is not just the present. A future is real. Without spontaneity and without creativity, the future would be just a repetition of what already was. The Exodus introduces the dimension of a radically new tomorrow. That is the idea of Messianism. The belief in a Messiah proclaims a radical futurism; a new separate concept in human consciousness of time. Life is not exhausted by endless cycles. **Once our story is told as our beginning through revolution, then history is a wide-open book.**

Jews have a crazy custom at the seder: They drink four cups of wine and then pour a fifth. They set the **cup of Elijah**, and fill it up. There is a chair waiting to welcome Elijah. The wine is poured, but not yet drunk. Yet the cup of hope is poured every year. Passover is the night for reckless dreams; for visions about what a human being can be, what society can be, what people can be, what history may become. That is the significance of "*Le-shanah ha-ba-a b'Yerushalayim*" (Next year in Jerusalem).

Memory and Values: On Family Education in the Modern World

■ by Rabbi David Hartman

(from *Joy and Responsibility*)

Any discussion of the family within a Jewish context must recognize the basic reality that **Judaism is fundamentally a *communal* spiritual system.** Judaism's distinctive institution, Halacha, is best understood within the categories of social order.

The law is not addressed to the individual seeking personal salvation; mitzvah is not designed for a mystical leap of the "alone" to the "Alone." The Torah is significant to the Jew who seeks spiritual fulfillment within the context of community. At Sinai "*all of you [stand] before the Lord your God — your tribal heads, your elders and your officials, all the men of Israel, your children, your wives, even the stranger within your camp, from woodchopper to waterdrawer."* (DEUTERONOMY 29:9-10) Individuals seeking spiritual answers do not gather at Sinai, but rather a whole people who already understand that they share a common historical destiny. They know a common fate and a shared suffering experienced in Egypt. The spiritual visions peculiar to this people emerge only after they are shaped as a collective entity. Halacha, legal obligation, may become meaningful for one's spiritual identity only if one acknowledges an organic relationship to a "we."

In the light of the above, the family in Jewish experience emerges against the background of a religious framework inextricably tied to community and to history. The collective nature of Jewish spirituality cuts across generations stretching from the distant past into the emerging future ("I make this covenant . . . not with you alone, but both with those who are standing here with us this day before the Lord our God and with those who are not with us here this day" (DEUTERONOMY 29:13-14). The family which is essentially the link between generations is of vital significance to this spiritual framework.

I. Four Challenges to the Modern Family

The modern family is challenged on four fronts, by technology, revolutionary universalism, despair and radical individualism.

Technological civilization has unleashed a spirit of looking to the future for salvation; technology promises something better for tomorrow, and encourages severance from the past. The technological human being prizes an ability to give up that to which one has become accustomed, and to adapt to that which is new. A vocabulary of commendation focuses on terms like "modern," "contemporary," "novel," "latest," etc. New possibilities, unthought-of ways of being happy, unprecedented means of material satisfaction, and the most recent modes of pleasure are, at once, descriptions and evaluations of the superiority of advertised products. In a technological society one is expected to be prepared for the unexpected.

Experience is characterized by a discontinuity in time. Events do not flow; there is no process of gradual, cumulative growth where the future carries the past within it. There are repeated radical new beginnings which destroy a sense of history. Technological persons are memory-less persons, for to remember is to connect the present to the past. To have a sense of continu-

ity and process is to attempt to build upon what is already there. Market technology, however, has come to represent shifting styles, new beginnings, and a ruptured perception of time.

In the area of human relationships this discontinuity is mirrored in the norm of defiance and breaking of ties. There is a positive attitude toward rebellion. The child who does not revolt deviates from the expected norm; failure to rebel requires explanation and analysis. Rebellion expresses the pervasive atmosphere of disjunction and rupture.

Furthermore, constant expectation and hunger for novelty have made permanent dissatisfaction a characteristic feature of modernity. If people are not discontented, they lose desire; and if they do not wish something other than what they have, what is the point of living? In order to desire the new, there must be a feeling of discontent, even an element of frustration. Against this background of dissatisfaction, there sometimes emerges a profound adult resentment against children's ability to immerse themselves in novelty, for in a technological society, one of the worst things that can happen to a person is to age; growing old deprives one of the ability to seek novelty and consume incessantly. At other times, in a very profound way, the child emerges as the vicarious redeemer. It has become a truism to say, "My child will have all that I lacked."

Young people growing up in a child-centered family become **persons without memories**, constantly in search of identity. "Who am I?" is the question that haunts this generation because part of the answer has to do with where one came from. The language of youth reveals the malaise: "I've got to put myself together," "I'm in pieces," "I feel lost." Even while driven by the search for the new, young people are internally frightened, because they do not know where a future severed from the past will lead. Modern people are in constant flux: they have to change; their eyes never rest; they exude an aura of freedom of motion. But at the same time, they suffer from profound fear and disquietude.

When there is no sense of history, and the past is felt to be superfluous, the family loses its centrality. **Parents are significant when the past is important;** if what happened before is of little interest and if memory is of no account, parents lose their value as adults. Thus one discovers in technological societies **a shift from the parent-centered to the child-centered family.**

Children emerge as the herald of a better future; they educate the parents as to what really counts. The juvenile messengers bring the news of tomorrow to a family without memory; since the dominant orientation is futuristic, they must teach about the new, unfolding world. Thus technological society not only promotes rupture and rebellion, it may also emotionally over-burden children by making them the final judges of the family's significance and direction.

A second challenge to the family is **revolutionary universalism**. The universalist "radical" often accuses the family of being provincial and restrictive, for commitment to a family supposedly diminishes one's concern with the greater community of humankind. To be loyal to a particular family is said to be confined and limited. When the dominant mode of consciousness is a single-minded hope for a universal new being, the family becomes an anachronism. When one believes that the future offers a thoroughly unprecedented solution to the problems of the human condition, anything that anchors one to the past becomes counterrevolutionary. The radical activist will reject loyalty to parents and to family if convinced that the future contains undreamed-of answers to the conflicts of humankind. The family, in such a revolutionist model, is totally obsolete.

On the other hand, people with memories and traditions are characteristically more conservative, because they know that reform is not that simple. The romantic utopians who believe that the future offers redemptive novelty hate anyone who points to doubts and difficulties. They despise talk about experience; they reject "old people" who speak about complexities and about the naiveté of believing in the creation of a "new human being" in history. One who operates with an illusion of utopian, apocalyptic novelty cannot have much regard for one's mother and father because, being from a prior generation, they represent the crumbling world of the past.

A third challenge to the integrity of the family derives from the opposite stance, from **pessimism and hopelessness**. Black despair and pervasive despondency grip college campuses which only a short while before were centers of militant activism. Instead of breaking windows and planning a radically new tomorrow, students turn inward to try and put themselves together.

A family is not reared on despair. A child is not born out of dejection. To create a home is in some way to believe in and feel responsible for the future. Despondency traps peo-ple within themselves, while longing for a child is an act of self-transcendence. Rootlessness casts off a family; hopelessness aborts it; and intoxication with the new as a radical solution subverts it.

Out of despondency, some individuals have salvaged the strength to search for a **radical individualism** in which each person is seen as infinite in one's own possibilities. Unbounded meanings are available within each person and there are no internal borders to what is possible. Uniqueness is a gift guaranteed at birth, and despair can be overcome by discovery of the individual soul. The subject of introspection is a bottomless abyss, unlimited, available to endless experimentation.

When radical individualism becomes the ultimate unit of human significance, when meaningfulness derives solely from the self, then the family is an intolerable burden.

II. Resources from the Tradition for the Modern Family

In the modern period, then, the family is challenged on four fronts. **Technology** confronts it with a sense of temporal discontinuity. **Utopianism** opposes it with its vision of disconnected, revolutionary possibilities. **Despair** robs the family of its child. **Radical individualism** annihilates familial roots and structures. Nevertheless, even in such an environment one must raise families and encourage children to marry and bear offspring.

There are no quick-and-easy solutions to complex social problems. Traditions, with all the reverence they deserve, do not mechanically provide formulas for the resolution of every human dilemma. "What's-your-problem? I-have-the-answer," is a childish misunderstanding of the relationship of a religious tradition to issues of modernity. Nonetheless, the Jewish tradition can suggest directions to take.

The following Talmudic list of parental duties suggests a model of goals and values realizable within a familial context. What follows is not a literal exposition of the text, but a transposition of traditional *halachot* (Jewish laws) into the contemporary situation. I shall accordingly examine specific *halachic* duties with an eye to their broader application to the role of the family.

What are the responsibilities of a parent to one's child? The Talmud imposes six obligations on a parent.

The father is bound in respect of his son, to **circumcise** [him],

12

redeem [him, if he is firstborn], **teach him Torah, take a wife for him**, and **teach him a craft**. Some say to teach him to swim too. *(T.B. KIDDUSHIN 29A)*

• *1) Circumcision*

The first duty is **b'rit milah**. The Jewish infant must be introduced into the covenant of Abraham. The task of the parent is to demonstrate that a Jew is the progeny not only of biological parents but also of a person, who thousands of years ago, entered into a covenant with God. Jews are the descendants of a person whose identity was not based upon family biology, but upon a complete transformation of values. Abraham is not defined exclusively by his past but by his spiritual conversion which showed him the way toward a universal dream.

> And I will bless them that bless you, and him that curseth you will I curse; and in you shall all the families of the earth be blessed. *(GENESIS 12:3)*.

> As for Me, behold. My covenant is with you, and you shall be the parent of a multitude of nations. Neither shall your name any more be called Abram, but your name shall be Abraham; for the father of a multitude of nations have I made you. *(GENESIS 17:4-5)*.

The symbolic significance of the change in name from Abram to Abraham is that recognition of Abraham as one's parent is not restricted to biological lineage but extends to participation in a certain way of life. The *b'rit* is a symbol of Jewish identity; a person is not defined by genetic constitution alone, but by norms and ideals. The Jew's first task as a parent is to bear witness to an identity beyond the chemical and the physical. The parent must introduce the child to the founder of the Jewish people. The family is not only a biological survival unit, but also a framework for developing identity grounded in the covenantal aspirations of Judaism.

Furthermore, **the *b'rit* of Abraham points to a human being able to defy a whole world.** In his legal code, *Mishneh Torah*, Maimonides presents a moving account of Abraham.

> The Creator of the Universe was known to none, and recognized by none, save a few solitary individuals. The world moved on in this fashion, till that Pillar of the World, the Patriarch Abraham, was born. After he was weaned, while still an infant, his mind began to reflect. By day and by night he was thinking and wondering: "How is it possible that this [celestial] sphere should continuously be guiding the world and have no one to guide it and

cause it to turn round; for it cannot be that it turns round of itself." He had no teacher, no one to instruct him. He was submerged, in Ur of the Chaldees, among silly idolaters. His father and mother and the entire population worshipped idols, and he worshipped with them.

> But his mind was busily working and reflecting till he had attained the way of truth, and knew that there is One God, that He guides the celestial sphere and created everything . . . He realized that the whole world was in error, and that what had occasioned their error was that they worshipped the stars and the images, so that the truth perished from their minds. Abraham was forty years old when he recognized his Creator.

> Having attained this knowledge, he began to refute the inhabitants of Ur of the Chaldees, arguing with them and saying to them, "The course you are following is not the way of truth." . . . When he had prevailed over them with his arguments, the king (of the country) sought to slay him. He was miraculously saved, and emigrated to Haran. *(HILCHOT AVODAH ZARA 1:2)*.

A child learns from Abraham of the strength and dignity to be an iconoclast in history. Abraham inspires one with the courage to say "no" to the corruptions of one's time. The ability to reject, of course, must not be a compulsion. A person who says "no" only because another says "yes" is but a conformist, since his response is defined by others. A person with convictions stands firm because of his values. A person in the iconoclast tradition of Abraham can stand alone in opposition to the environment out of profound conviction and love for a particular way of life. This "no" grows out of one's own "yes."

• *2) Redeeming the First Born*

The second duty, ***pidyon ha-ben***, the redemption of the first born son at the age of 30 days old, indicates that the parents must not merely bring their children into the covenant of Abraham, but must introduce the child to the memory of Egypt. The child must remember that "We were slaves to Pharaoh in Egypt" and that the first born were struck down. Therefore each first born must be redeemed in the ceremony of *pidyon ha-ben*.

> When your child asks you in time to come, saying: What is this? You shall say: By strength of hand the Lord brought us out from Egypt, from the house of bondage; and it came to pass, when Pharaoh would hardly let us go, that the Lord slew all the first-born of humans, and the first-born of beast; therefore I sacrifice to the Lord all that opens the womb, being males; but all the first-born of my sons I redeem. And it shall be for a sign upon

12

your hand, and for frontlets between your eyes; for by strength of hand the Lord brought us forth out of Egypt. *(EXODUS 13:14-16).*

One of the most important functions of parents is transmitting a knowledge of reality outside the child's experience. The father and mother must provide frames of reference rooted in the memories and the history of the covenantal community of Israel. **The task of the parent goes beyond entering the child's world; it is to expose the children to a domain reaching beyond their own.**

Halakhah demands *yir'ah* (awe) for parents. *Yir'ah* expresses distance. The parent is never wholly accessible. The children are faced with a reality that comes to them from outside of their world. Their identity is not grounded in their experience alone; it is enriched by memories and by a past that is mediated by their parents. One of the essential tasks of the parent is to relate previous history; the parent is a story-teller who narrates a world the children never knew.

A primary source for evil according to Jewish tradition is the loss of memory. Those who do not build upon their memory and who are frightened and ashamed of their past may manifest hostility towards others because their sense of worth and dignity is derived only by manipulation and control of others.

The poor people who prevail through difficult struggles to attain wealth, and then block out the memory of their past become harsh taskmasters. "Self-made men" can be sensitive to others only when they are unashamed to talk about their former destitution. If they cannot bear the thought of their former poverty, they will act with cruelty to those who remind them of their former degradation.

In recalling Egypt, the Jews are exhorted to remember that they were once slaves. Rather than deny it, they are to incorporate that slavery into their consciousness. Thus, love the stranger because you too were outcasts in Egypt; have regard for the poor because you too were once servants; care for the oppressed because you too were persecuted; aid the crushed because you know what it means to face extermination; be cautious with power because you have suffered the perversions of another's might.

When the prophets seek to return the Jewish people to moral conduct, they attempt to restore its memories. Socrates believed that the source of evil was ignorance: virtue is knowledge. The prophets, however, identified evil with loss of historical memory.

A sense of historical memory provides the children with a filter through which they can evaluate their own experience. They need not be inextricably bound to modernity because other life-options are present in their consciousness. The given need not be perceived as inevitable and necessary, because they are aware of patterns of life other than what they experience at the moment. **Historical memories sharpen and develop a critical posture towards modernity.**

The parent is the link that ties the children to the story of their past. The role of parents is to develop in the identity of the child a sense of history, a temporal consciousness, an empathy for a whole world of experience that was not theirs. Whether these memories are relevant and meaningful, and how the child will live by them, are different issues. **The mother's and father's task is not to decide how the children will use their memories. Their obligation is to see to it that the child does not enter into the future without a past.** This is the familial significance of *pidyon ha-ben.*

• 3) *Teaching Torah*

Having elaborated upon educating children into covenantal and historical solidarity with their people in Egypt, the Talmud then states the third obligation, **to teach Torah**. The tradition viewed the family not only as a link to that which was, but also as the transmitter of values to guide the children in their everyday life.

The mitzvah of learning Torah is central in the Jewish tradition. *"The ignorant person cannot be pious."* (PIRKEI AVOT) Knowledge is essential for spiritual growth. The biblical sentences enunciating the commandment to learn Torah are set within a familial structure, *"And you shall teach them to your children."* (DEUTERONOMY 6) The Talmud, however, understands the term "child" to refer not only to children in one's family but one's students as well. *"To your children.* (DEUTERONOMY 6:7) These are the disciples. Everywhere do we find that disciples are termed *banim* [children]."* (SIFREI, DT., PISKA 23)

According to the Halacha, each person sufficient in knowledge — whether parent, grandparent, or teacher — is commanded to impart wisdom to their charges. Although Maimonides subsumes parent and child, and teacher and student, under the same rubric of "and you shall teach them to your children," he distinguishes between the parent and the teacher in terms of priority. One's child has priority over one's

12

student. Parents are also required to sacrifice economically to find a teacher for their offspring, but they are not so obliged regarding those who are strangers.

Even though the tradition permits transference of the role of parent-as-teacher to the more formal educational framework of teacher-student relationship, there nevertheless remains unique significance in the role of **parent-as-teacher**. The parent imparts information and in addition creates a living environment which embodies educational values. Values are not only transmitted through formal learning but also through the living and intimate community of the family.

A teacher in a formal school setting need not build a common commitment with his pupils. Shared learning does not require shared existential solidarity. Thus, the danger of formal education is that the student may perceive a gap between life and learning. **For the child to recognize the intimate bond between learning and action ("great is learning because it leads to practice") and sense that ideas make a difference in the way one builds a life, one needs parents seriously committed to their role as educators.**

A further possible distinction between the educational role of the family and formal schooling concerns the relationship between learning and ethical responsibility. A school achieves its goal if it instills in the student intellectual curiosity. Schools cultivate intelligence and seek to introduce the child to the ocean of the Talmud, with its logical intricacies and subtle distinctions. The joy of intellectual creativity and of being totally engaged in a difficult passage of Talmud may lead to the severing of the intellectual personality from the ethical responsibility. The family, however, relates learning to mitzvah. Familial education enriches the personality of the child by teaching that learning for its own sake loses its significance if it does not enhance one's sensitivity to one's normative obligations.

Moreover, the parent is more a living model for the child. Moral education is restricted if one's source of norms derives only from textbooks. Law and morality, however cognitively convincing they may be, are incomplete if they do not grow out of living images that concretize and embody values. In moments of crisis, one derives the strength to overcome weakness and temptation not only from one's critical reasoning powers, but also from **"significant others"** who have impressed themselves upon one's consciousness. **Parents as living models can instill courage in moments of crisis.**

When Joseph was managing the household of Potiphar in Egypt, his master's wife, struck by Joseph's ability and good looks, tried to seduce him. A Talmudic account relates that at one point Joseph was about to succumb to her enticements. At this moment of truth, he did not recall the prohibition against adultery, but rather he saw the image of his father, Jacob and he fled her grasp. Joseph's decision to uphold his loyalty to his master was not so much the result of the normative force of certain rules, as the compelling influence of the memory of his father. The image of the parent concretizes the claims of the past.

It is interesting to observe that, halakhically, the teaching of Torah was a command addressed not only to parents but also to **grandparents**. The Talmud finds biblical support for the role of grandparents in *Talmud Torah* in the text *And you shall make known to your children and your children's children the day you stood at Horeb.* (DEUTERONOMY 4:9-10) One might teach one's children Torah in order to help them find immediate meaning and guidance for everyday living, for the teachings of Torah are *our lives and length of our days and we shall meditate on them day and night.* On the other hand, Torah is also to be studied in order to introduce the children to their deeper, collective historical roots. This kind of teaching might be the task of the grandparents, for they are, symbolically, closer to the historical moment of Sinai. Grandparents can relate instruction not simply to the present and future, but also imbue study of Torah with a sense of continuity from Sinai.

Learning blossoms beyond the desire of pupils for guidance in their own lives; it also expands a sense of responsibility to the normative dreams of the community of Israel. The intellect becomes saturated with historical commitments. **Not only is Torah study a quest for self-realization, it is also an attempt to place the individual within the covenant of Israel's collective existence.**

- ### *Parental Duties regarding*
  ### *4) Marriage;*
  ### *5) Professional Training; and*
  ### *6) Survival Skills*

We have discussed three foci of the Jewish heritage: the covenant (*berit milah*), Egypt (*pidyon ha-ben*) and Sinai (*Talmud Torah*). The Talmud adds that parents must find their children a spouse (CF. JER. 29:6) and teach them a trade (CF. ECCL. 9:9).

The attention paid to marriage in Tractate Kiddushin indicates a concern with the body of the child. It is the responsibility of parents to recognize that their children have physical and emotional needs. Moral education which ignores the reality of the physical is abstract and unreal.

Thus the *bar mitzvah* of a boy is at age thirteen, and the *bat mitzvah* of a girl at age twelve since, according to the Talmud, sexual maturity is reached by a boy at thirteen, and by a girl at twelve. Normative responsibility is related to sexual development. Self-awareness and moving outside of one's self should not only be expressed in instinctual physical development but also in the capacity to assume responsibility for oneself and for others.

The duty to provide for the marriage of one's children is not to be understood solely in economic and physical terms, but indicates the importance of creating family conditions which foster the psychological capacity to love. The task of modern parents, broadly speaking, is to build a family structure which instills feelings of adequacy enabling the mature son or daughter to function in the framework of marriage.

With regard to the obligation of teaching one's child a trade, there were two opinions expressed in the Talmud: one was to teach a child any business, and another, that of Rabbi Judah, was to teach him to be a skilled artisan so as to withstand the fluctuations of the market. The goal is to provide the child with a source of economic dignity and strength so as not to be overwhelmed by financial stress or upheaval.

The last obligation, to teach the child how to swim, in some way implies that part of the role of the parent is to teach and help the child to cope with unpredictable circumstances and events. Do children know how to handle sudden crises? Can they meet emergencies? Are they crushed by unanticipated changes in their lives?

Thus, the parent must instruct the children how to deal with critical situations. Similarly, the children should be able to handle economic problems and must feel the dignity of being able to support themselves and to earn a living. In sum, **Halakhah obligates the parent to cultivate in the child psychological adequacy, economic know-how, and competence.**

Perhaps a parent may wonder whether achievement of a sense of psychological competence and of economic independence will undermine the children's need for their parents. It is true that economic and emotional dependence on parents often constitutes the link which keeps the parent-child relationship alive. Many a parent feels that independence constitutes a threat to their significance *vis-à-vis* their children.

The Talmud aimed at creating independent children. Concerning everyday life, the Rabbis were not afraid to develop psychological and economic self-sufficiency in offspring. Halachic Judaism did not encourage economic dependency; nor did it wish to burden children with paralyzing emotional feelings of guilt and shame, which block the ability to love and respond openly to others. Neither did the Talmud fetter children to parents by fear of crises and stress.

Providing a Legacy of Memories

The family in the halachic framework is meant to be an instrument of history; the parent is significant for the child not because of the latter's helplessness and incompetence, but because, without the parent, the child has no Sinai, no Egypt, no Abraham, i.e., no memory. When the family loses its significance as a source of history, it centers increasingly on dependency ties; helplessness becomes the ground of human relationships. In such a family the parents may feel needed only because their children cannot survive tomorrow without them. **In the tradition-oriented family, they may feel needed because the next generation cannot live in the future without a past.**

Judaism imposes a vital task on the parents: to tell the children their people's story. What the child does with this past, no parent can decree. **Parents provide their children with luggage.** Whether the child will open up the suitcases and use their contents is beyond the reach of parents. They have no right to enter the child's future. Parents must aim at instilling memories that haunt the child an entire lifetime; their bequest is a weight of generations, an awareness that one's biography began with Abraham and Sarah.

12

❧ Chapter 13
Exploring Exodus

■ *by Nahum Sarna*

The newly founded community of Israelites in Egypt prospered at first, and their numbers grew enormously in the course of the years. The divine promises to the patriarchs that their posterity would be numerous were amply fulfilled. The Israelites had become a "great nation." As the text has it, they "were fertile and prolific; they multiplied and increased very greatly, so that the land was filled with them." The term "land" here most likely refers to the area of their settlement, the region of the eastern part of the Nile Delta, not to Egypt as a whole. This population explosion was perceived as a threat and a danger to the security of Egypt, and when a "new king," most probably the founder of a new dynasty, took over the reins of power, the situation came to a head.

If the anxieties of the authorities were understandable in the circumstances, the reaction to the potential menace posed by **the presence of a large foreign population in a strategic area** can only be described as iniquitous. The Pharaoh took draconian measures to limit the growth of the Israelites, and to this end he cunningly devised that adult males be pressed into slavery.

The pharaoh involved is not identified. The term "Pharaoh" itself simply means in Egyptian **"The Great House."** Originally applied to the royal palace and court, late in the XVIIIth Dynasty it came to be employed by metonymy for the reigning monarch, just as "The Palace" or "The White House" or "City Hall" would be used today. This is how it is employed in the Bible. If the pharaoh in question belonged to the XIXth Dynasty, the new policy of dealing with the Israelites coincides with known events belonging to this period.

In other words, **Rameses II** built his capital in the very area of

Israelite settlement. Not only so, but this pharaoh achieved an unrivaled reputation as a vigorous **builder** on a prodigious scale. Monumental structures, numerous obelisks, colossal statues of himself, magnificent palaces and temples adorned the land of Egypt, and especially the Delta, in the course of his sixty-six year rule.

State Slavery

Such vast public projects required an unlimited supply of labor, a high degree of organization, and the continuous production of abundant supplies of brick, masonry, and other building materials. The pharaoh could find a large pool of manpower at hand in the Delta in the Israelite population, and he proceeded to exploit it to the full.

So they set taskmasters over them to oppress them with forced labor; and they built garrison cities for Pharaoh: Pithom and Raamses.

What we are dealing with is **state slavery**, the organized imposition of forced labor upon the male population for long and indefinite terms of service under degrading and brutal conditions. The men so conscripted received no reward for their labors; they enjoyed no civil rights, and their lot was generally much worse than that of a household slave. Organized in large work gangs, they became an anonymous mass, depersonalized, losing all individuality in the eyes of their oppressors.

They were requisitioned for the maintenance of the irrigation ditches, dikes, and canals, having to clean out the mud deposited by the inundation of the Nile. Agriculture in Egypt is not sustained by rainfall, which is too meager for the purpose, but by the annual rise of the Nile, which is literally the lifeline of the country. A ramified network of ditches and canals conducts the Nile waters into the fields. Unless these waterways are constantly kept in proper condition, the fertile soil becomes barren.

13

---

*Prof. **Nahum Sarna** is author of* Understanding Genesis, Exploring Exodus, *and the* JPS Commentary on Genesis, Exodus. *The selection here concerns Exodus chapters 1-2.*

The building program inaugurated by Rameses II required an inexhaustible supply of bricks. The lives of the Israelites were "embittered with harsh labor at mortar and brick." From another episode it becomes clear that they were required to manufacture the bricks according to fixed daily quotas.

Something of the hardships experienced by the brickmaker may be perceived from an inscription accompanying wall paintings from the days of Thutmosis III (ca. 1490-1436 B.C.E.). It depicts, among various scenes of building construction, Asiatics making and laying bricks, and it bears the ominous line from the mouth of a taskmaster, "The rod is in my hand, do not be idle." The "Satire on the Trades" has this to say of the brickmaker and the builder: "He is dirtier than vines or pigs from treading under his mud. His clothes are stiff with clay; his leather belt is going to ruin. Entering into the wind, he is miserable … His sides ache, since he must be outside in a treacherous wind … His arms are destroyed with technical work … What he eats is the bread of his fingers, and he washes himself only once a season. He is simply wretched through and through …."

Civil Disobedience

The nefarious scheme of the Pharaoh to reduce the male Israelite population through state-imposed enslavement and its subjection to degrading, exhausting, and backbreaking toil, did not yield the expected results: "But the more they were oppressed, the more they increased and spread out." *(EXODUS 1:12)* Accordingly, the king resorted to more barbarous measures. In order to achieve immediate and certain regulation of the population, he decreed the murder of all new-born Israelite males. The obligation to commit this infanticide was thrust upon the midwives.

What is remarkable is that the names of these lowly women are recorded whereas, by contrast, the all-powerful reigning monarch is consistently veiled in anonymity. In this way the Biblical narrator expresses his scale of values. All the power of the mighty pharaoh, the outward magnificence of his realm, the dazzling splendor of this court, his colossal monuments — all are illusory, ephemeral and, in the ultimate reckoning, insignificant, and they must crumble into dust because they rest on foundations empty of moral content. Seven times in this brief episode *(EXODUS 1:15-22)* the term "midwife" is repeated, an index of the importance that Scripture places upon the actions of the women in their defiance of tyranny and in their upholding of moral principles.

The midwives, fearing God, did not do as the king of Egypt had told them; they let the boys live.

Here we have history's first recorded case of civil disobedience in defense of a moral cause. Be it noted that the motivation of these women in defying the promulgated law of the sovereign is given as "fear of God." This term is frequently cited in biblical texts in relation to situations that involve norms of moral or ethical behavior. It will be recalled that in Genesis 20:11 Abraham justified the tactic he adopted, of passing off his wife as his sister in order to save his life, on the grounds that the local citizenry was not thought to possess "fear of God," and would not, therefore, have any restraint on committing murder. Joseph sought to convince his brothers of his integrity by appealing to his own "fear of God." In Leviticus 19:14, 32, one is exhorted not to insult the deaf or place a stumbling block before the blind, to rise before the aged and to show them deference — all out of "fear of God." The Amalekites could commit unprovoked aggression against the peaceful Israelites who had just escaped from Egyptian bondage because "they had no fear of God." Job was a perfectly righteous man who eschewed evil precisely because he did "fear God." In short, the consciousness of the existence of a Higher Power who makes moral demands on human beings constitutes the ultimate restraint on evil and the supreme incentive for good.

Faced with an irreconcilable conflict between obedience to the sovereign's depraved law and allegiance to the higher moral law of God, the midwives chose in favor of the transcendent imperative of morality. Their noncompliance with the law, however, was not publicly announced but privately effected on obvious prudential grounds. They could not disclose the truth in response to the pharaoh's interrogation because had they done so, the predictable consequence would have been their removal from a situation in which they could be enabled to save lives.

Thwarted once again in his evil designs, the pharaoh now enlists "all his people," the entire apparatus of the state, in a national effort systematically to annihilate the people of Israel. All new-born males are to be drowned in the River Nile, a decree that is ultimately to turn out as tinged with irony, for the very agency of destruction that he has chosen — water — is eventually to become the instrument of his own punishment.

13

The Birth of Moses

The facts are simple enough. A Levite family has a son. Because of the pharaoh's decree, the infant is hidden away for three months, but the situation becomes intolerable and the mother fashions a wicker basket, caulks it with bitumen and pitch, and places the baby therein among the bulrush at the Nile's edge. His sister stands nearby to keep watch. The pharaoh's daughter happens to come by, notices the basket, and has it fetched. When opened, it was seen to contain a crying baby, which the princess recognized at once to be an abandoned Hebrew child. At that moment the sister approaches and offers to bring a Hebrew nurse, to which the princess readily agrees. Thereupon the pharaoh's daughter unwittingly hires the infant's own mother as a wet nurse. When the child is weaned he is delivered to the princess, who adopts him and names him Moses.

This simple narrative is spiced with conscious irony directed against the king. The course of history hinges upon a single event — the rescue of Moses — and it was brought about by the daughter of the very tyrant who decreed Israel's extinction! To add to the effect, Moses' natural mother is actually paid by the palace to rear her own child! In the end, the Egyptians bestowed their bounty upon the departing Israelites.

Aside from the irony, there are stylistic features that are meant to arouse immediate associations that disclose a certain understanding of events. We are told that Moses' mother "saw that he was good (tov)." This phrase is usually taken to mean that he was "a goodly/fine/handsome child." Literally, the Hebrew simply translates **"She saw him that he was good."** Now this statement recalls a key phrase in the Genesis creation story — **"God saw that it was good"** — occurring there seven times, and one wonders whether, by repeating it here, there is not a deliberate attempt to stir an echo of that chapter, to inform us that the birth of Moses is another Genesis, an event of cosmic significance. What is more, the "wicker basket" in which the baby is laced is called in the Hebrew, **tevah.** This noun is used again in the Hebrew Bible only in the story of Noah and nowhere else, and it is employed in that context because it is an ark, not a sailing vessel; that is to say, like Noah's ark, our tevah is the instrument of salvation in the perilous waters, though it possesses neither steerage gear nor steersman, being wholly dependent upon God's benevolent protection for its safety.

The container that held the infant Moses was placed among the "reeds," in Hebrew **suf**, a term borrowed from the Egyptian for "papyrus/reed thicket." The idea of the mother was to make sure that the infant would not be carried downstream. It may well be that the rare word suf has been selected in the present text because it is allusive, prefiguring Israel's deliverance at the Sea of Reeds (Hebrew: yam suf).

The Role of Women

An interesting feature of the Exodus narrative is the favorable light in which the daughter of the wicked pharaoh is portrayed. Her name is not given. If her father was indeed Rameses II, she would have been one of his fifty-nine daughters! Her motive for saving the crying baby is sincere and honorable; she is actuated by pity. Indeed, the story is remarkable for the prominent, fateful, and generally noble role played by women — the midwives, the mother, the sister, the Egyptian princess, and soon, Jethro's daughters.

It should not be considered strange that the king's daughter conducts the negotiations and concludes the transaction regarding the care of the infant entirely by herself, without the assistance of husband or other male. The social and legal position of the woman in Egypt was relatively high. Descent was strictly matrilineal, so that property descended through the female line. This meant that the woman possessed inheritance rights and could dispose of property at will. As a result, she enjoyed a certain measure of economic independence.

The particular arrangements that the princess made for the nursing and rearing of the child follow a pattern found in Mesopotamian legal texts that relate to the adoption of a foundling. These "wet-nurse contracts," as they are now called, provide for payment for the services of suckling and rearing the infant in the home of the wet nurse for a specified period, usually two to three years. Following the weaning, the child is returned to the finder, who then adopts it. This deferring of the adoption until after the weaning is probably to be explained by the high infant mortality rate. The Laws of Hammurabi, #194, make provision for just such a contingency — that the baby might die when in the care of a wet nurse — so it could not have been a rare occurrence. The documents dealing with these contracts derive from Mesopotamia, not Egypt. It is probable, though not certain, that there was a common practice in such matters throughout the Near East.

The Name "Moses"

The princess named the child "**Moses**" following her formal adoption of him. She explained, "I drew him out of the water." As is frequently the case in the Bible when names are given an etymological explanation, what we really have is word-play. In the present case, the pharaoh's daughter obviously bestowed an Egyptian name on the child, which has been artfully interpreted as a Hebrew word from the stem מ-ש-ה, "to draw out (from the water)," itself exceedingly rare in biblical vocabulary. The meaning of the name as a Hebrew verb is "the one who draws out," an active form, whereas a passive, "the one who was drawn out" (Hebrew: mashui), would be expected. We may surmise that once again the narrative is subtly pointing to Moses' destiny as the one who safely led Israel to freedom across the Reed Sea. In actual fact, the name that the princess conferred upon the child is of Egyptian origin. It has as its base the verb משי, "to be born," or the noun מש, "a child, son," frequent elements in Egyptian personal names, usually with the addition of a divine element. Examples are Ah-mose, Ra-mose, Ptah-mose, Thot-mose — in each case meaning "The (god) X is born." Names such as these would be given to babies born on the anniversary of the god's birthday according to the local mythology. Sometimes the second element alone appears as an abbreviated name. A papyrus from the Rameside era records a grievance against a vizier that is lodged before a certain "Mose" who was powerful enough to depose the vizier. Another inscription from the time of the XIXth Dynasty deals with a court proceeding concerned with land ownership in which the plaintiff's name is Mose. In light of these facts, it is quite clear that the king's daughter gave the Hebrew child an Egyptian name, which the biblical narrator has reinterpreted in terms of a Hebrew verb, thereby hinting scornfully that the pharaoh's own daughter unwittingly has rescued the one who will eventually deliver his people from her father's oppression. She has given him a name that foreshadows his destiny.

Moses' Upbringing

The narrative is silent on the years Moses spent in the palace, which is where he undoubtedly passed the formative period of his life. Like the other privileged boys in royal court and bureaucratic circles in Egypt, he would have commenced his education at the age of four, attending school from early in the morning until noonday for about twelve years. Discipline is known to have been exceedingly strict, with corporal punishment the chief means of its enforcement. One notable proverb frames the educational theory thus: *"The ears of a boy are on his back; he hears when he is beaten."* The school curriculum largely centered on reading, writing, and arithmetic, the second of these subjects receiving special emphasis. The art of penmanship and the cultivation of style were both highly esteemed as the indispensable prerequisites for a sound education. Drill and memorization seem to have been the chief pedagogic techniques.

As far as Moses is concerned, the likelihood of his having received such a conventional education as was achieved by the sons of the privileged is enhanced by the substantial evidence from the period of the Ramesides for the presence of foreigners, especially of Semites, in the royal schools. Notwithstanding the knowledge and the skills that Moses acquired as the adopted son of the Egyptian princess, one thing is certain: it was the values and the beliefs of his parental home that remained paramount in his life. He was seized with the consciousness of his Israelite identity: *"... when Moses had grown up, he went out to his kinsfolk and witnessed their labors."*

Three Tests of Moses's Character

Three incidents in his life that occurred while he was still attached to the palace are given prominence in the narrative because they reveal aspects of his character and disclose his commitments. Having *"witnessed the labors of his kinsfolk"* and become sensitive to their sufferings, he cannot tolerate the sight of an Egyptian beating a Hebrew. This outrage against decency and human dignity spontaneously arouses in him feelings of anger and resentment. He strikes down the oppressor and buries him in the sand. By this act Moses has decisively thrown in his lot with his suffering people and has psychologically severed his ties to his aristocratic and privileged Egyptian past. His instinctive indignation at the maltreatment of his brethren has effectively overcome his self-interest.

The narrative does not relate to the moral questions that may be raised concerning Moses' fatal blow against the Egyptian oppressor, because the function of the story in the present context is to illustrate prime qualities of Moses' character and personality — his intolerance of oppression and his whole-hearted identification with the plight of his people. In any case, the facts are too meager to permit any valid moral judgment. For instance, we do not know whether the Egyptian seemed to

13

be actually beating his victim to death, in which case Moses' intervention was in accordance with the elementary human duty of going to the aid of one whose life is in peril. Significantly, the same Hebrew verb, *hikkah*, "to strike," is used for the action of the tormentor as for the reaction of Moses. Certainly the story does not lend itself to any interpretation that seeks to find in the incident a justification for the use of violence as an instrument to achieve what may be viewed as a desirable end. There is no ideology of protest at work in the story, and Moses is not praised for his deed. There is only a tale about an isolated event, an impetuous and spontaneous outpouring of righteous indignation in response to a specific situation. The counter-assault was directed against the perpetrator of the atrocity, not indiscriminately aimed against anyone who is perceived to be a symbol of the coercive power of the state.

In the **second incident**, Moses encounters two Israelites who are quarreling, one of whom raises his hand against his fellow. Moses remonstrates with the bully, once again evincing instinctive sympathy for the underdog. However, from the assailant's retort it becomes clear that the story of Moses' attack on the Egyptian is common knowledge. He is now a wanted man, condemned to death by the authorities, and he flees for his life into the wilderness to take refuge in the territory of the Midianites. There he sits down by a well. Wells in the Near East often served as meeting places for shepherds, wayfarers and townsfolk, and it was natural for a newcomer to gravitate toward them. Abraham's servant had gone straight to the well on arriving at Haran, and Jacob did the same thing at the end of his flight from his brother, Esau, to his Uncle Laban.

Here at the well, Moses experiences the **third test of his character**. He witnesses rough local shepherds pushing aside a group of girls who were first in line to draw water. Once again he cannot remain indifferent. His spirit rebels against the abuse of the weak by the strong. He cannot tolerate this blatant infringement of the girls' rights, and he immediately rises to their defense, driving off the offending shepherds, and himself watering the girls' flock. Their father, described as "the priest of Midian," invites the rescuer home, and Moses ends up marrying one of his daughters.

Of Moses' life in Midian, nothing is known except that the urbane Israelite, reared in the royal palace, pursued the shepherd's life just as his ancestors had done. [One day in the wilderness he came across a burning bush. That is the most critical test of Moses' character — his willingness to be called back to Egypt and fulfill the Divine mission. — *Editors*]

13

≋ Chapter 14
Exodus and Revolution

■ *by Michael Walzer*

The House of Bondage and Political Liberation

Egypt was called a "house of bondage" (literally: house of slaves). What features of the house of bondage do we highlight when we describe it as tyrannical? What specifically were its unjust impositions? Why did Egyptian bondage become the original and archetypal form of oppression?

The easiest modern reading of the first chapter of the Book of Exodus is social and economic in character; we are accustomed to think of oppression in those terms. Lincoln Steffens provides a nice example when he calls Moses a "loyal labor leader." A contemporary Latin American priest describes the suffering of the Israelites under four headings: **repression, alienated work, humiliation,** and **enforced birth control**. That last phrase might refer to a midrashic story according to which the Egyptians worked their male slaves so hard and long that they could not return to their wives at night but fell asleep, exhausted, in their workplaces. Or it might refer to Pharaoh's order to the midwives to kill the newborn sons of the Israelites. This is **infanticide**, not birth control; its purpose was to destroy the entire people of Israel by destroying the male line, leaving a population of women and girls to be dispersed as slaves among Egyptian households.

Among Jews it has come to be seen as the first of a series of attempts on Jewish peoplehood that culminates in the Nazi death camps. Indeed, the Pharaoh of the oppression does sound oddly like a modern anti-Semite, worrying *(IN EXODUS 1:10)* about the growing power of the Israelites, who had prospered in Egypt,

In Exodus and Revolution *(Basic Books, 1985) distinguished political philosopher* **Michael Walzer** *(Princeton University) describes how the Biblical story of bondage and liberation in Egypt became a major paradigm for Western culture. Oppressed people and classes turned to the Bible for much of their moral rhetoric and self-understanding.*

and their possible disloyalty: *"lest they join our enemies . . . ."* But it isn't the killing of the sons that figures in the earliest discussions of the Exodus story in Deuteronomy and the Prophets.

The central tradition focuses on the *corvée*, not on the attempted genocide. *"And they made their lives bitter with hard bondage, in mortar, and in brick, and in all manner of service in the field; all their service, wherein they made them serve, was with rigor."* *(EXODUS 1:14)* The Hebrew word for "with rigor" is *be-farech*, and it occurs only one other time in the Torah, in Leviticus 25, where the laws for the treatment of Israelite slaves are laid down: *"Thou shalt not rule over (them) with rigor,"* that is, as the Egyptians did. Many years later Maimonides effectively extended this protection to all slaves, and at the same time he offered a definition of be-farech. Rigorous service, he suggested, is service without the limits of time or purpose. **Bondage involves work without end; hence it is work that both exhausts and degrades the slave**. Writing in the sixteenth century, the author of the *Vindiciae* takes a similar view: the tyrant, he says, "erects idle and needless trophies to continually employ his tributaries, that they might want leisure to think on other things, as Pharaoh did the Jews . . . ." Because of what Pharaoh did, perhaps, Biblical legislation sets a limit on the term of enslavement — though a limit that applies only to Israelite slaves: *"If you buy a Hebrew servant, six years he shall serve: and in the seventh he shall go out free for nothing."* *(EXODUS 21:2)* We don't know if the limit was ever enforced, but it was not forgotten. The prophet Jeremiah blames the fall of Judea and the Babylonian exile on the failure of the people to "proclaim liberty" to enslaved brothers and neighbors after six years, as they had covenanted to do, he says, when God brought them up out of Egypt. *(EXODUS 34:8-23)* It may be that the freedom of the seventh day — an easier matter — was more widely accepted than the freedom of the seventh year. In Deuteronomy, the reason given for the establishment of the

14

Sabbath is "that your manservant and your maidservant may rest as well as you ... remember that you were a servant in the land of Egypt." *(DEUTERONOMY 5:14; SEE ALSO EXODUS 23:12)* This commandment includes all slaves, not only Israelites but also "strangers." It is based, no doubt, on a certain view of physical and spiritual needs but also on the memory of the degraded character of "rigorous" slavery. **Alienated work** and **humiliation** do capture at least part of the oppressiveness of Egyptian bondage.

One might, alternatively, understand *be-farech* in the sense of **physical cruelty**. Here, too, the laws proclaimed immediately after the escape from Egypt, where the Israelites had been beaten and killed, seem designed to rule out Egyptian oppression: *"And if a man hits his servant or his maid ... and he die under his hand; he shall surely be punished. (EXODUS 21:20)* Slave-owners who kill their slaves are not "put to death," as in the case of ordinary murder *(EXODUS 21:12)*, so this isn't quite the "absolute equality of slave and free man in all matters regarding the judicial safeguarding of their lives ...." Still, the safeguards established by the Exodus prohibitions have "no parallel in either Greek or Roman law." Moreover, if a slave suffered physical injury at the hands of his master, he was to be set free. *(EXODUS 21:26-27)* Again, we don't know if these laws were enforced, or how consistently they were enforced, during different periods of Israel's history. But they are Exodus laws, and they presumably express the Israelite understanding of their own suffering in Egypt.

Egyptian bondage was the bondage of a people to the arbitrary power of the state. Chattel slavery was conceivably preferable, for it was a condition governed by legal norms. **In "the house of slaves," there were no norms.** The Israelites were submitted to a bondage without limit — without rest, without recompense, without restraint, without a purpose they might make their own. In Egypt, slavery was a kind of political rule. Of course, Pharaoh profited from the work of his Israelite slaves, but he did not enslave them for the sake of the profit. The slaves were exploited, as all slaves are, but it is more important in the Biblical account that they were oppressed, that is, ruled with cruelty, ruled tyrannically. The Exodus tradition speaks against **tyranny** and that is the way it figures, for example, in the preaching of Savonarola, in the pamphlets of John Milton, and in American revolutionary sermons attacking the "British Pharaoh."

The memory of the Exodus is more often invoked on behalf of aliens than on behalf of slaves: *"You shall not oppress a stranger: for you know the heart [nefesh: "spirit" or "feelings"] of a stranger, seeing you were strangers in the land of Egypt." (EXODUS 23:9)* It is easy to understand why the Exodus story appealed so much to African slaves in the American South. Though these were chattel slaves, they were also aware of themselves as a separate people, **strangers in a strange land**, who shared a common fate. Egyptian bondage is paradigmatic for abolitionist politics, and for radical politics generally, because of its collective character. It invites a collective response — not manumission, the common goal of Greek and Roman slaves, but liberation.

We can think of the Exodus as an example of what is today called **national liberation**. The people as a whole are enslaved, and then the people as a whole are delivered. At the same time, however, the uses of the story in Israel's own history — first in legislation and then in prophecy — suggest that the Egyptian model reaches to every sort of oppression and to every sort of liberation.

Benjamin Franklin's proposal for the Great Seal captures the political sense of the Exodus text. Franklin uses Moses leading the Hebrews across the Red Sea as a symbol of America's battle against English tyranny. Franklin went beyond the text, however, with his proposed inscription: "Resistance to tyrants is obedience to God." *(See Haggadah page 121.)*

Flesh Pots: The Seductive Attractions of "Egypt"

Bondage and oppression are the key ideas in the Exodus story, but the analysis of these ideas does not exhaust the significance of Egypt. No old regime is merely oppressive; it is attractive, too, else the escape from it would be much easier than it is. The attractions of Egypt don't appear very plainly in the text, but they figure necessarily in the interpretation of the text, that is, in efforts to expand upon and explain the foreshortened, often enigmatic narrative.

We can best begin, though, with a well-known passage from chapter 16 of the Book of Exodus. The Israelites have been in the wilderness now for forty-five days.

> And the whole congregation of the children of Israel murmured against Moses and Aaron ... And the children of Israel said, would that we had died by the hand of the Lord in the land of Egypt, when we sat by the fleshpots and when we did eat bread to the full .... *(EXODUS 16:2-3)*

I first read this passage years ago, when I was very young, and focused then, as I shall do now, on that wonderful word **"fleshpots."** My attention was drawn, I confess, rather to the first part of the word than to the second; in fact, I don't remember thinking about the second at all. Nor did I ever firmly grasp, until I began working on this book, just what a fleshpot was. A prosaic object, a pot for cooking meat: even in the United States today, we sit, or most of us do, by our fleshpots. But my adolescent preoccupation with the flesh was on the mark, for meat throughout most of human history has been the food of the privileged, and "fleshpots," in the plural, doesn't refer to a lot of pots but to luxuries and sensual delights.

This became the standard view so that generations of reformers have railed against Egyptian luxuries. Ernst Bloch takes the luxuries to be outsized and tawdry, the mirror image of modern consumer culture: "Mammoth Egypt ... the shoddy product and symbol of the world that has come to be." In the eyes of Savonarola, Florentine "vanities" simply repeated Egyptian luxuries. Preaching on Exodus, he stressed the rich and lascivious life of the Egyptians; the promised land, the new society, would be different. The Jewish historical and interpretive literature takes a similar line. One rabbinic commentary argues, against the apparent meaning of the text, that when Pharaoh issued his command to the midwives, he was "as much interested in preserving the female children as in bringing about the death of the male children. [The Egyptians] were very sensual, and were desirous of having as many women as possible at their serve. Josephus writes in the same vein in his *Antiquities of the Jews*: "The Egyptians are a nation addicted unto delicacy and impatient of labor, subject only to their pleasures ...."
In these passages, we can hear the note of disapproval that is missing in the people's complaint about the fleshpots (though not, of course, in the narrator's report of the complaint or in Moses' reply: "Your murmurings are not against us but against the Lord"). The note of disapproval is sounded much more strongly in Leviticus and Deuteronomy and then by the Prophets. "After the doings of the land of Egypt, wherein ye dwelt, you shall not do." *(LEVITICUS 18:3)* **Early Judaism is defined by its rejection not only of Egyptian bondage but also of Egyptian culture:** the customary ways of the upper classes as they ate and drank, dressed and housed themselves, amused themselves, worshipped their gods, and buried their dead.

Egypt was a center of wealth and good living; it makes sense to suggest that many Israelites admired the very people who oppressed them, copied Egyptian ways, curried Egyptian favor. And other Israelites feared and repressed the impulse to act similarly themselves.

The Exodus: A Paradigm for Revolution

Since late medieval or early modern times, there has existed in the West a characteristic way of thinking about political change, a pattern that we commonly impose upon events, a story that we repeat to one another. The story has roughly this form: oppression, liberation, social contract, political struggle, new society (danger of restoration). We call the whole process *revolutionary,* though the events don't make a circle unless oppression is brought back at the end; intentionally, at least, they have a strong forward movement. This isn't a story told everywhere; it isn't a universal pattern; it belongs to the West, more particularly to Jews and Christians in the West, and its source, its original version, is the Exodus of Israel from Egypt.

The Book of Exodus together with the Book of Numbers is certainly the **first description of revolutionary politics**.

The Exodus, or the later reading of the Exodus, fixes the pattern. And because of the centrality of the Bible in Western thought and the endless repetition of the story, the pattern has been etched deeply into our political culture. It isn't only the case that events fall, almost naturally, into an Exodus shape; we work actively to give them that shape. We complain about oppression; we hope (against all the odds of human history) for deliverance; we join in covenants and constitutions; we aim at a new and better social order. Though in attenuated form, Exodus thinking seems to have survived the secularization of political theory. Thus, when utopian socialists, most of them resolutely hostile to religion, argued about the problems of the "transitional period," they still cast their arguments in familiar terms: the forty years in the wilderness were "a deep ... cultural memory and the death of the old generation [was] an archetypal solution." Cultural patterns shape perception and analysis too.

The Exodus parallel was not lost on the most impressive of Zionist thinkers, Ahad Ha-am ("One of the People," the *nom de plume* of Asher Ginzberg), who published an essay on Moses in 1904. This is a powerful piece, describing a leader who imagined at first that liberation would be immediate and complete but who learned in the wilderness that it would be a long and hard struggle. Ahad Ha-Am repeats **Maimonides: "A people trained for generations in the house of bondage cannot cast off in an instant the effects of that training and become truly free . . . ."** And he has Moses draw the conclusion that he himself drew with regard to his own contemporaries: He no longer believes in a sudden revolution; he knows that signs and wonders and visions of God can arouse a momentary enthusiasm, but cannot create a new heart, cannot uproot and implant feelings and inclinations with any stability or permanence. So he summoned all his patience to the task of bearing the troublesome burden of his people and training it by slow steps till it is fit for its mission.

So pharaonic oppression, deliverance, Sinai, and Canaan are still with us, powerful memories shaping our perceptions of the political world. The "door of hope" is still open; things are not what they might be — even when what they might be isn't totally different from what they are. This is a central theme in Western thought, always present though elaborated in many different ways. We still believe, or many of us do, what the Exodus first taught, or what it has commonly been taken to teach, about the meaning and possibility of politics and about its proper form:

- **first, that wherever you live, it is probably Egypt;**
- **second, that there is a better place, a world more attractive, a promised land;**
- **and third, that "the way to the land is through the wilderness." There is no way to get from here to there except by joining together and marching.**

14

Chapter 15

'Here Am I' — A Personal Midrash on Moses' Search for Identity

■ *by Julius Lester*

The story of Moses' beginning is familiar — his birth during the time Pharaoh decreed death to newborn male Hebrews, his concealment by his parents for three months, his being placed finally in a basket of reeds by the bank of the Nile, and the discovery of him there by Bithiah (the rabbinic name for Pharaoh's daughter).

Pharaoh's Daughter "Opens Up"

The question must be asked: Why did God give the responsibility for his rearing to an Egyptian woman and the daughter of Pharaoh? Who was this woman and what did she impart to Moses?

I can imagine a young woman dissatisfied with the life and values bequeathed her by her father. It was a life without substance, though every physical need was filled and every material desire satisfied. She has reached that critical moment in life where dissatisfaction has become unbearable and action is required. The only problem (and it is always the problem): she doesn't know what to do. It is at such times that God presents us with an opportunity to act, if we recognize it as such.

She sees a basket among the reeds beside the river. The closed basket looks like a tiny coffin. Does it contain the body of a dead Jewish boy? She does not turn and walk away from the possible horror, but orders the basket brought to her. The midrash records that one of the slave girls said:

Julius Lester, a social activist and a scholar in Afro-American studies who discovered his Jewish family origins, converted to Judaism and became a professor of Jewish studies at the University of Massachusetts. This essay appeared in New Traditions, *Spring 1984.*

Your Highness, it is the general rule that when a king makes a decree, his own family will obey that decree even if everyone else transgresses it; but you are flagrantly disobeying your father's command?

Yes, because her need for identity separate from her father was much greater.

The basket is brought to her and instead of ordering the slave girl to open it, Bithiah knows that she must be responsible for her act, and the text records this remarkable line: *"And she opened it, and saw it, even the child."* (EXODUS 2:6)

What is this "*it*" she sees even before she sees the child?

The crucial word in the line is "opened." To open is one of the most important and difficult spiritual acts we are asked to do. Only when we open can the new present itself. But **opening** means forsaking the comfort and knowledge of the familiar to enter the unknown, whose parameter and shape is not yet revealed.

When we truly open, we see, and we see that we see. It is the conjunction of objectivity and inner clarity and comes only after we have the courage to risk inner turmoil of unbearable proportions. This conjunction is an experience of the Shechinah (the Divine Presence), which is the "it" Bithiah sees.

Moses' Dual Identity

Sometime after that, when Moses had grown up, he went out to his kinsfolk and witnessed their toil. He saw an Egyptian beating a Hebrew, one of his kinsmen. He turned this way and that and, seeing no one about, he struck down the Egyptian and hid him in the sand. (EXODUS 2:11-12)

What kind of spiritual transformation can come from

15

an act of murder? What has ensued in the years between Moses' being taken to live in Pharaoh's palace and this act?

The text does not tell us, but it is not difficult to imagine. Abraham Ibn Ezra and Martin Buber, among other Jewish commentators, note that it was important for Moses to be raised as Bithiah's son because it enabled him to escape being inculcated with the slave mentality of submissiveness. The physical oppression of slavery creates a corresponding intellectual and spiritual oppression. Reb Simha Bunam of Pshiskhe (1765-1827) observed that the greatest evil of the Egyptian exile was that the Israelites were able to tolerate anything . . . when the Lord saw them toiling away with mortar and bricks and patiently resigned to their slavery, He said to Moses, "If they can tolerate this, things are bad, and we have to get them out of Egypt soon, otherwise they will be slaves the rest of their lives." Their redemption began when they ceased to tolerate their slavery.

Being free, Moses was not prey to the slave psychology. However, growing up as Pharaoh's grandson thrust him into an equal danger — the ambivalence of **dual identity**. He was Hebrew and Egyptian. By birth he belonged to the oppressed, but he was nurtured as a member of the oppressing group. It is wishful thinking to assume that Moses was immune to the comforts and privileges of his station in life.

Still, there must have been times when Moses felt like a traitor to his people, especially as he relaxed on a hot day, a fine robe draping his body, servants offering him pomegranates, figs, and dates, while his people worked in the hot sun building pyramids. I wouldn't doubt that sometimes Moses wept in silent helplessness as he tried to unravel the dilemma of appearing to be an Egyptian while knowing himself a Jew. He is a stranger in Egypt and a stranger to himself because he cannot live his true identity.

Nothing is so vital to psychological well-being as identity. Through identity we know our place in the world. If that identity is seriously divided or defined by a society as negative, we are insecure in the world and insecure in ourselves. Moses was possibly the first person in history to have to ask, "Who am I?" Everyone else in the ancient world knew; they were Egyptian, Canaanite, Sumerian, slave, etc. They knew because society conferred identity on them and provided a place for them. **Moses had no alternative but to confer identity on himself.**

His first attempt to do so comes when he goes to face the suffering part of himself in the persons of his enslaved people. He looks on their "burdens" and weeps, saying "Woe is me for you! Would that I could die for you." *(MIDRASH RABBAH)* He feels their suffering as his own, because neither he nor they have identities that can confer on them an objective and subjective wholeness. It is a moment of intense compassion, charged with the emotion of a life-and-death conflict. And because true compassion compels one to act, he does. He kills an Egyptian.

What did Moses hope to accomplish by this isolated act of violence? Did he expect the Jews to see what he had done and rise up to overthrow their oppressors? Obviously not, because the text tells us that he looked around to make sure he wasn't seen before he committed the murder. At the very least, his act was politically misguided and ineffectual. **What, then, is the relationship between the murder and his identity?**

It is ironic that murder can be crucial in the process of self-transformation. And Moses must transform himself before he can undergo the more excruciating process of spiritual transformation. I do not speak of murder in the literal, physical sense, but psychologically, as when we "kill" a hated part of ourselves. Unfortunately, most of us carry out these murders on the persons of those around us. Anti-Semitism, racism, and sexism are all psychological acts of murder directed outward against Jews, blacks and women. Sometimes such "murders" are acted out politically, as in the sixties when blacks perpetrated a verbal violence on whites because whites represented what blacks had come most to despise in themselves.

Such acts are necessary but are only efficacious when we recognize that the "enemy is us" and we eschew the luxury and convenience of an enemy who is "them." But God did not allow the Hebrews who made the exodus from Egypt entrance to the Promised Land, because they did not kill the Egyptians in themselves.

Moses' act of murder is, therefore, crucial to his identity, but he projects his self-hatred outward onto one who most closely resembles that hated Egyptian part of himself. Notwithstanding Moses' very real compassion for the suffering Hebrew, his act is unintelligent. Why didn't he use his influence as Pharaoh's grandson to effect change? Joseph had not even been a member of the royal household, but his influence was profound. But Joseph had no identity problem. Moses is in a state of crisis. He wants to be a part of his people, and murdering an Egyptian was the way to come home.

It was not, and Moses knew it immediately, because he hides the body in the sand. He does not brag about what he had done or call others to come see, exhorting them to do the same.

I imagine him looking at what he has done. His rage at the injustice of oppression, his rage at his own impossible non-identity passes quickly as he stares down at the man who a moment before was a living human soul. He feels no exultation, no sense of freedom or wholeness. Instead, he is engulfed by remorse, shame, and guilt. He is more of a stranger now than he could have ever imagined possible.

The sense of strangeness intensifies the next day when he returns to the scene of the crime and sees two Hebrews fighting. Watching them he learns that not only do the oppressors abuse the oppressed, but the oppressed abuse each other. When he stops the fight, one of the men asks him if he intends to kill them as he did the Egyptian. Moses thought no one knew. His act is known and it inspires contempt.

Moses is a stranger now in Egypt, a stranger to his people, and a stranger to himself, and it is with this strong sense of dissociation that he flees to Midian. At a well there he confronts and beats shepherds who are harassing the seven daughters of the priest of Midian who have come to draw water for their sheep.

In this instance his sense of **compassion** — what Buber calls "the protection of the weak from the power of the strong" — is effective. Compassion must be wedded to judicious action if it is not to degenerate into self-righteousness. Moses does not kill the shepherds, but merely drives them away, which is all the situation requires.

The daughters run to tell their father what happened:

An Egyptian delivered us out of the hand of the shepherds, and moreover he drew water for us and watered the flock. (EXODUS 2:19)

One stops and re-reads the lines to be sure the eye has not made a Freudian slip. Moses is not an Egyptian. Why do the daughters call him that?

The answer is obvious. He has come from Egypt and is dressed, therefore, like an Egyptian. Of course he would be so mistaken. Jewish legend is not so accepting. It says that Moses stood outside the tent and heard himself described as an

Egyptian and that he did so "without protesting and asserting his Hebrew birth. For this God punished him by causing him to die outside of the promised land."

Elie Wiesel gives another reason for Moses' concealing his identity. He says that **Moses fled Egypt after killing the Egyptian, not because he feared Pharaoh, but because he was disgusted that the Jews "were not worthy of the freedom he wanted for them."** When the daughters of Jethro mistook him for an Egyptian, he did not protest because "he was a hidden Jew in search of assimilation."

Both assessments overlook the **agony of double identity**. Perhaps Moses' refusal to correct them comes neither from any denial of his Jewishness nor from a desire to assimilate. Is it possible that he has not resolved his identity problem?

What does Moses know about being Jewish? He has grown up in Pharaoh's palace. One can assume that he has had an education worthy of Pharaoh's grandson. He knows that he is Jewish, but his knowledge is intellectual only, because he has not shared the lives of Jews. He does not know their suffering in his flesh. Yet, his intellectual knowing is strong enough to keep him from assimilating. He is a Jew, but one of a new order precisely because he has not known the burdens and the bondage. Thus, he cannot tell Jethro's daughters that he is a Jew because he does not know yet what this means for him.

He marries Zipporah, one of the seven daughters, and becomes a shepherd. Does this mean he retreats from defining himself as a Jew? Perhaps. His efforts at identity have failed. He has run away from his suffering people. He must feel he is **a personal and political failure**. Unlike Bithiah, Moses' spiritual transformation does not begin in turmoil but in a deep and abject emptiness. This is as it should be. As it is written: *"The Lord is near unto them that are of a broken heart."* (PSALM 34:19)

"Here Am I" at the Burning Bush

Is it here that Moses' process of spiritual transformation begins in earnest. He becomes a shepherd and in shepherding he learns to tend, to care for, because his life will be one of tending and caring for the Jewish people. But before he can assume that enormous responsibility, he must learn to shepherd his own soul.

I imagine Moses with the sheep in the vast silence of the land, day after day. Nothing is perhaps more cleansing, more healing, than solitude and silence. And there is much that needs healing

15

in him. He must stop wondering why he was burdened with a dual identity. He must have time and silence in which to let the memories fade — how the Nile looked at sunset from his suite of rooms at the palace, the fatherly old scribe who taught him hieroglyphics. How exhilarating it was to watch a royal falcon wheel and turn in the sunlight. He must let the silence and the solitude swallow all of it while he tends to his shepherding. And there he will uncover the deeper level of being a stranger, that level on which he will become a stranger to the world in order to be known by God. As it is written: *"You are strangers and settlers with me."* (LEVITICUS 25:23)

Eventually the memories fade, and thinking has left him exhausted. There is nothing now but the sheep and the silence. He settles into the silence and is healed, but without knowing it yet.

Then, one day he takes his sheep *"to the farthest end of the wilderness"* where he comes *"to the mountain of God, unto Horeb."* (EXODUS 3:1) He sees a bush on fire, but the bush is not consumed by the fire.

> And Moses said: *"I will turn aside now, and see this great sight, why the bush is not burnt."* And when the Lord saw that he turned aside to see, God called unto him, out of the bush, and said: *"Moses, Moses."* And he said, *"Here am I."* (EXODUS 3)

Moses sees a burning bush that does not consume itself and he does not exclaim, "What the hell is that?" Nor does he disbelieve the evidence of his senses and say, "That can't be! There's something wrong here." Neither does he scoff and say, "That's weird." He says "I will turn aside now and see this great sight."

I will turn aside now. Why "now?" Had he been staring at the bush for some time before deciding finally to go closer? Clearly, because he could not have known otherwise that the bush was not being consumed by the flames.

But why does he say, *"I will turn aside?"* Where was he going that he had to turn aside? The text tells us that he came to the mountain of God, which means that he was not going to it intentionally. He was wandering around in the desert with the sheep and came to the mountain of God and did not know that it was the mountain of God. He was probably going to wander right past it, and God had to flag him down with a miraculous burning bush.

"I will turn aside now," he says. It is his moment of **opening**

and it is fused with seeing, for Moses turns aside, not to examine or state incredulously, but *"to see this great sight."* It is as if he knows what it is he is seeing and he is not afraid. As with Bithiah, objective seeing and inner clarity are conjoined.

"I will turn aside now," he says, and turning aside is a conscious and deliberate choosing, because the very next line says: *"And when the Lord saw that he turned aside to see, God called unto him."* He turns aside, leaving the normal course of his dailiness, and opens to the Divine Presence. It is as if all God needs is for us to turn aside and see: When we do, God is there, calling our names. Moses turns, and God sees that he has chosen and calls his name twice.

Moses responds with the simple and eloquent, **"Here am I."** Once again, two actions are fused into an inseparable whole. "Here am I" is the decisive action to which his cleansing, opening, and seeing lead. God calls his name and he responds immediately. This is absolutely remarkable! A voice calls his name from the midst of a burning bush that is not being consumed, and Moses does not question his sanity or wonder if he has spent too much time in the sun or with the sheep. He says, "Here am I."

To say "Here am I" is not the same as "I am here." The latter is a statement of existence. "Here am I" is an affirmation of being. It can be said only when you are centered in yourself, naked and unshielded before God.

When Moses says, "Here am I," his identity dilemma is resolved. His process of spiritual transformation is complete. He is a Jew, but a new kind of Jew, and to him will be revealed the Divine Name, the Tetragrammaton. To him will be given the Torah and the Law.

Only someone divided within himself would be compelled to become one, and because he is one, as God is One, he can stand before the burning bush and answer the call of his name, **"Here am I."**

15

Chapter 16
Moses and Herzl

■ by David Golinkin

LILLIEN'S DESIGN FOR A STAINED GLASS
WINDOW OF "MOSES" IN WHICH HE USED
THE HEAD OF HERZL

Ephraim Moses Lilien (1874-1925) was a popular Jewish artist and illustrator at the turn of the century. He was also an ardent Zionist who corresponded with Theodore Herzl, attended the Zionist Congresses and even took the famous photo of Herzl on the Basel Bridge. Lilien illustrated many books, among them a 1912 edition of the bible. In that bible there is a dramatic illustration of Moses breaking the two tablets of stone in which Moses bears a striking resemblance to Herzl. That identification, however, is not conclusive because later on in the same bible Aaron too looks somewhat like Herzl and, in another illustration by Lilien, Herzl is portrayed as an angel! Nevertheless, Lilien also designed a stained glass window for the B'nai Brith of Hamburg in which he placed the head of Herzl on the torso of Moses.

More importantly, on at least two occasions, Herzl *himself* thought he was somehow connected to Moses. Half a year before his death, Herzl told Reuven Brainin the following story. At about the age of twelve, he had read somewhere in a German book about the Messiah who would come riding on a white ass in order to redeem the Jewish people. A little while later, Herzl had the following dream:

> "The King-Messiah came, a glorious and majestic old man, took me in his arms, and swept off with me on the wings of the wind. On one of the iridescent clouds, we encountered the figure of Moses. The features were those familiar to me out of my childhood in the statue of Michelangelo. The Messiah called to Moses: It is for this child that I have prayed. But to me he said: Go, declare to the Jews that I shall come soon and perform great wonders and great deeds for my people and for the whole world."

Rabbi David Golinkin is an Associate Professor of Halacha at the Seminary of Judaic Studies (The Bet Midrash) in Jerusalem of the Masorti (Conservative) Movement.

At a later point in his life, Herzl seems to have identified with Moses in a much more direct fashion. In March of 1898, already feeling the financial and physical strain of his Zionist activities, Herzl put down the outline of a biblical drama, "Moses." He envisioned Moses as

> "a great, powerful figure, filled with the strength of life and the spirit of humor. The drama is to show how he becomes inwardly grim, while retaining his will to the full. He is the leader because he does not want to be it. Everything is swayed to his will because he has no personal desires. His aim is not the fulfillment, but the wandering... Aging, he encounters and recognizes Korah [and] the golden calf, the eternal characteristics of slaves. All these things weary him, and yet he must urge the others forever forward with fresh energy. It is the tragedy of a leader of men who is not a misleader...."

It does not require a psychoanalyst to determine that Herzl is really talking about himself.

Lastly, we have the reaction of his contemporaries. Chief Rabbi Moritz Gudemann of Vienna also compared Herzl to Moses. On August 17, 1895 Herzl read him the first draft of his "Address to the Rothschilds" which later became "The Jewish State." That evening, Gudemann said to Herzl:

> "'It is as if I saw Moses in the flesh... Continue to be that which you are. Perhaps you are the one who has been called by God?' And he kissed him."

16

Yet even without this contemporary evidence, a careful reading of the respective biographies of Moses and Herzl yields a series of striking parallels between them in terms of education, character, plans and ultimate success.

1) Age

Let us begin with the age at which they became involved with the "Jewish Problem." According to one well-known midrash, Moses was forty years old when he revealed himself to his oppressed people. Similarly, Theodore Herzl was 35 years old in June of 1895 when he went to lay his proposal for a Jewish state before Baron Maurice de Hirsch.

2) Education

Moses was brought up in the house of Pharaoh. (EXODUS 2:10) We tend to think of him as an observant Jew, but this, of course, is an anachronism. In truth he must have been quite assimilated. His name Moses is a typical Egyptian name. Moses must have also *looked* like an Egyptian, because when he saved Jethro's daughters from the Midianite sheperds, they went home and told their father: "An *Egyptian* man saved us from the shepherds." (EXODUS 2:19) Furthermore, when his firstborn son Gershom was born, he neglected to circumcise him with almost disastrous results. (EXODUS 2:22 AND 4:24-26) Lastly, the New Testament reports that "Moses was learned in all the wisdom of the Egyptians." (ACTS 7:22)

Herzl was not brought up in the house of Pharaoh, but he too grew up in an atmosphere far from Jewish tradition. Although he attended the Liberal synagogue across the street from his home in Budapest and had his Bar Mitzvah there, his parents were quite assimilated and German culture was clearly much more important to them than Jewish culture.

3) The Spark

Given their backgrounds, there was no logical reason for Moses and Herzl to become involved with the plight of their people. Moses could have continued to live a coddled life in the house of Pharaoh, while Herzl could have continued his successful career as the Paris correspondent of the *Neue Freie Presse* of Vienna. What sparked their involvement in the "Jewish problem?" What made them return to the Jewish fold with a vengeance? It appears that they both had an innate hatred of injustice and an innate desire to help the downtrodden. The story of Moses's leaving the House of Pharaoh is encapsulated in

seven verses (EXODUS 2:11-17), yet in those seven verses he manages to get involved with three fights that were none of his business. First he intervenes when an Egyptian is beating a Hebrew (v. 11-12). Then he gets involved when a Hebrew is fighting with another Hebrew (v. 13-14) and, finally, he saves the Midianite daughters of Jethro from other Midianites (v. 15-17). In other words, Moses was a man who could not bear the sight of injustice. He could not sit on the sidelines. When one human being — whether Jew or Gentile — mistreated another, he had to get involved. As Ahad Ha'am so eloquently stated:

> "The Prophet has two fundamental qualities which distinguish him from the rest of mankind. First he is *a man of truth*. Secondly, the Prophet is an *extremist*. From these two fundamental characteristics there results a third, which is a combination of the other two: namely, the supremacy of absolute *righteousness* in the Prophet's soul, in every word and action . . . .

> "When Moses first leaves the schoolroom and goes out into the world, he is at once brought face to face with a violation of justice and, unhesitatingly, he takes the side of the injured. Here, at the outset, is revealed the eternal struggle between the Prophet and the world . . . .

> "Then 'two Hebrews strove together . . . .' Once more the Prophet's sense of justice compels him, and he meddles in a quarrel which is not his . . . [He is forced to flee to Midian] . . . before he has had time to find a friend and shelter, he hears once more the cry of outraged justice, and runs immediately to its aid. This time the wranglers are not Hebrews, but foreigners and strangers. But what of that? The Prophet makes no distinction between man and man, only between right and wrong. He sees strong shepherds trampling on the rights of weak women — 'and Moses stood up and saved them.'"

And what of Herzl; what triggered his involvement in the Jewish problem? It is true that beginning in 1892 he became more and more interested in the plight of his people and dealt with anti-Semitism in his letters, his newspaper reports and his play "The Ghetto." But in 1893 he still believed that the real and definitive solution could only lie in the complete disappearence of the Jews through baptism and intermarriage. The spark that ignited his Zionism and propelled him to write "The Jewish State" was the public degradation of Captain Alfred Dreyfus on January 5, 1895. Herzl was present at that event in his capacity as a reporter and he heard the mob shout *"A mort les Juifs!"* — "Death to the Jews!" Like Moses, he could not bear the sight of injustice, especially of injustice against an innocent Jew. As one of his biographers writes,

> "... the ghastly spectacle of that winter morning must have shaken him to the depths of his being. It was as if the ground had been cut away from under his feet. In this sense Herzl could say later that the Dreyfus affair had made him a Zionist."

4) The Plan

Moses's plan was very simple: "Thus says the Lord, the God of Israel: Let my people go ...." *(EXODUS 5:1)* At God's behest, he wanted to take the Jewish people out of slavery, and lead them to Eretz Yisrael. Herzl had a similar plan. He wrote in his "Address to the Rothschilds" in 1895: "This simple old idea is *the Exodus from Egypt*. When he went to see Baron Maurice de Hirsch in June 1895, he said to him:

> "I will say to the German Kaiser: *Let us go forth*. We are aliens here, they do not let us dissolve into the population, and if they let us, we would not do it. *Let us go forth*."

And he later wrote in his diary: "I pick up once again the torn thread of the tradition of our people. *I lead it to the Promised Land.*"

5) The Reaction of the Jewish People

When Moses and Aaron went to visit Pharaoh for the first time they were rebuffed. Instead of freeing the People of Israel to celebrate a festival in the wilderness, Pharaoh cracked down on them. From now on, their quota of bricks would remain the same, but they would have to gather the straw themselves. The Israelite foremen took out their wrath on Moses and Aaron: *"May the Lord look upon you and punish you for making us objectionable to Pharaoh and his courtiers — putting a sword in their hands to slay us." (EXODUS 5:21)* In other words, they had a typical slave mentality: stay out of trouble and you'll survive. Later on, Moses tells his people God's promise of deliverance. *"But when Moses told this to the Israelites, they would not listen to Moses, their spirits crushed by bondage." (EXODUS 6:9)*

Herzl, too, was initially rejected by the Jewish people. On June 2, 1895 he went to see Baron Maurice de Hirsch, one of the richest men of his time and the founder of the Jewish Colonization Association (ICA) which had already colonized 3,000 Jews in Argentina. Baron de Hirsch cut Herzl off in the middle of the conversation. Herzl then wrote in his diary a sixty-five page

pamphlet entitled "Address to the Rothschilds." He decided to read it to his friend Friedrich Schiff. When Herzl finished, he asked Schiff for his reaction. Schiff replied that he considered the plan the product of an overstrained mind and he urgently advised Herzl to take a rest and seek medical treatment.

Later, Herzl read his "Address" to Chief Rabbi Moritz Gudemann of Vienna and Heinrich Meyer-Cohen, a Zionist from Berlin. Meyer-Cohen expressed sharp opposition and declared the entire plan a Utopia of the fantasy. Gudemann was at first taken with the plan, as noted above, but he soon changed his mind and published an article decrying the "*Kuckucksei*" (cuckooness) of Jewish nationalism.

In November 1895, Herzl went to Paris to see Narcisse Leven, general secretary of the Alliance Israelite Universelle, and Chief Rabbi Zadoc Kahn. They too rejected his plan.

Finally, Herzl published the revised version of his "Address" under the title "*Der Judenstaat*" ("The Jewish State") in February of 1896. Stefan Zweig later recalled the reaction of the Jewish middle class of Vienna:

> "I can still remember the general astonishment and annoyance of the middle class Jewish elements of Vienna. What has happened, they said angrily, to the otherwise intelligent, witty and cultivated writer? What foolishness is this that he has thought up and writes about? Why should we go to Palestine? Our language is German and not Hebrew, and beautiful Austria is our homeland ... Why does he who speaks as a Jew and who wishes to help Judaism, *place arguments in the hands of our worst enemies* and attempt to separate us, when every day brings us more closely and intimately into the German world."

This reaction sounds familiar. The reaction of the Jews of Vienna to Herzl is almost a paraphrase of the reaction of the Israelites to Moses 3,000 years earlier!

6) Hesitation and Doubts

Both Moses and Herzl were, at first, taken aback by the opposition of the very people whom they had come to save. After being berated by the Israelite taskmasters, Moses turns to God and says: *"O Lord, why did you bring harm upon this people? Why did you send me? Ever since I came to Pharaoh to speak in your name, it has gone worse with this people; yet you have not delivered your people at all." (EXODUS 5:22-23)* And again in the next chapter, when the Israelites refuse to listen to Moses, he turns to God and

16

says: *"The Israelites would not listen to me; how then should Pharaoh heed me, a man of impeded speech!"* (EXODUS 6:12)

Herzl, too, was devastated by the reaction of his friend Friedrich Schiff. On the very next day, he wrote a letter to Baron de Hirsch:

> "My last letter calls for a conclusion. Here it is: I have given the whole thing up. There is no helping the Jews for the time being. If someone were to show them the Promised Land, they would treat him with contempt. They are disintegrated. And yet I know where salvation lies: in us! ... But we shall have to descend deeper, we shall have to fall lower, we shall have to endure more insult ... before we become ripe for the idea ... We have not yet reached the right degree of despair. That is why the savior will be greeted with laughter."

7) Insanity

Of course, from an objective point of view, both the Israelites and Friedrich Schiff were absolutely correct: Moses and Herzl *were* insane. Moses had no army and no weapons — he barely had a people — and yet he appeared before Pharaoh, the greatest monarch of his day, and demanded: "Let my people go!" What unmitigated chutzpah! There was no reason for him to succeed and, yet, succeed he did.

Herzl was just as insane. He traveled to Constantinople in June of 1896. The Sultan at that time owed Turkey's creditors the incredible sum of 106 million pounds. Herzl let it be known that if the Jews were given Palestine as an independent state, they would undertake the regulation and normalization of Turkish finances and liberate the country from foreign control. There was only one hitch — Herzl did not have a penny in his pocket nor did he have the backing of Hirsch or the Rothschilds or Montagu who could have financed the scheme. Again, what chutzpah, and again he succeeded nonetheless.

8) The Personal Price

Moses and Herzl both succeeded. Their crazy dreams became reality. Moses took a group of slaves, made them a people and brought them to the threshold of their own land — all in the course of forty years. Herzl took a people scattered throughout the world for 1,800 years, reminded them that they *had* a land, and inspired them to return to it — all in the course of nine years.

Yet they both paid a heavy price. Moses was allowed to see the Promised Land but not to enter it.[33] Herzl visited the Promised Land in 1898, but did not live to see his vision fulfilled. He burned himself out and died of heart disease in 1904 at the age of 44. On his deathbed he said: "Give them all my greetings, and tell them that I have given my heart's blood for my people."

9) Why Did They Succeed?

We have no real way of knowing why Moses and Herzl succeeded in their impossible dreams. We can only hazard a guess. First of all, they both seem to have been handsome men with tremendous personal charm and charisma.

We, of course, do not have any portraits of Moses. But he was clearly very strong; he killed the Egyptian with one blow and he saved Jethro's daughters from the shepherds. (EXODUS 2:11-17) A number of sources emphasize Moses's *physical* beauty. Philo reports that "the child from his birth had an appearance of more than ordinary goodliness." When Pharaoh's daughter discovered him in the bullrushes, "she approved of his beauty and fine condition" and after he was weaned "he was noble and goodly to look upon." Josephus concurs and he adds that

> "When he was three years old, God gave wondrous increase to his stature; and none was so indifferent to beauty as not, on seeing Moses, to be amazed at his comeliness. And it often happened that persons meeting him as he was borne along the highway turned, attracted by the child's appearance, and neglected their serious affairs to gaze at leisure upon him ...."

The sages of the Talmud, however, were more interested in his *spiritual* characteristics:

> "The sages say: at the time when Moses was born, the entire house became filled with light. It is written here (EXODUS 2:2) 'And [his mother] saw *that he was good'* and it is written there (GENESIS 1:4) 'And God saw the light *that it was good.'*"

As for Herzl, we needn't rely on oral and written traditions. One merely has to look at a photograph of him to be impressed by his physical beauty and amazing eyes. And indeed, his contemporaries made frequent reference to his striking appearance.

But this could not have been the only reason for their success. After all, there have been many handsome and charismatic leaders who have failed in their chosen missions. There must, then, have been other, deeper reasons for their success. Ibn Ezra gives two such reasons for Moses's success in his commentary to

Exodus 2:3:

> "Perhaps God caused him to be raised in the royal house so that his soul would be on a higher plain through training and habit and not lowly and accustomed to being in the house of slaves … And another thing, because had he grown up among his brothers and had they known him from his youth they would not have been afraid of him for they would have related to him as one of them."

In other words, Moses succeeded because he grew up in Pharaoh's house and absorbed there both self-confidence and nobility. Had he been brought up as a slave among his people, he would not have had the self-confidence necessary to defy Pharaoh. Furthermore, the Israelites paid attention to him and gave him more respect because he came to them from the outside. They must have thought: if Moses who grew up in the house of Pharaoh is willing to redeem us from slavery, we should at least give him a chance and listen to what he has to say.

These same two explanations fit Herzl to the tee. Since he grew up in an assimilated German-speaking household, he did not have many of the feelings of inferiority so common among East European Jews who were consistently persecuted and treated as second-class citizens. More importantly, he was particularly popular among East European Jews who couldn't get over the fact that a successful, assimilated Viennese Jew had decided to devote his life to solving their problem. As Chaim Weizman explained:

> "Fundamentally, *The Jewish State* contained not a single new idea for us … yet the effect produced by *The Jewish State* was profound. Not the ideas, but the personality which stood behind them appealed to us. Here was daring, clarity and energy. *The very fact that this Westerner came to us unencumbered by our own preconceptions had its appeal.*"

That is why the Jews of Sofia, East London, and especially Vilna came out to greet him in droves and hailed him as their "Leader" and "King."

10) Conclusions

Thus far we have seen that there are a number of striking parallels between Moshe Rabbeinu and Theodore Herzl. They both grew up and were educated in a non-Jewish or assimilated atmosphere and discovered the "Jewish Problem" relatively late in life. Their devotion to their people was sparked by their reaction to an act of injustice and cruelty. Their plan of returning the Jewish people to their land was almost identical. The initial reaction of the Jewish people and their initial discouragement were also very similar in nature. Both of them advocated a plan which was impractical and insane and yet both plans succeeded. But they both paid a heavy personal price for their efforts; their plans succeeded but they did not live to enjoy the fruit of their labors. Lastly, their success can be attributed to three factors: their appearance and charisma, their noble upbringing and the fact that they were outsiders.

What lesson can we learn from the careers of Moses and Herzl? We learn the power of one individual to change history. Without Moshe Rabbeinu we might still be slaves to Pharaoh in Egypt. God sent Moses and God performed signs and wonders in the land of Egypt, but without the human leadership of Moses neither Pharaoh nor the Jewish people would have listened. Similarly, without Theodore Herzl the Zionist movement and the State of Israel would never have come into being. Hovevei Zion and Rothschild would have continued their settlement work, but the massive waves of *aliyah* which led to the founding of the State of Israel would probably never have occurred.

Like Moses and Herzl before them, it is the outsiders who come to Israel from afar who have the ability to dream dreams and to work miracles.

The footnotes have been deleted and the conclusions abbreviated with the author's consent. The complete article is found in *Conservative Judaism*, Vol. 47 No. 1, Fall 1994, pp. 39-49.

16

☙ *Permissions*

We thank all those who granted us use of their creative work and we apologize to all those whom we were unable to locate to request permission.

Cover page — Ira Steingroot, by permission of Harper Collins ©1995

Chapter 2 — Lawrence Halprin, *RSVP*

Chapter 4 — Ilene Vogelstein, early childhood educator, Chizuk Amuno Synagogue, Baltimore, MD and Marcelle Zion contributed many ideas to this chapter.

Chapter 7 —
- Dr. Joel Ziff, *Mirrors in Time*, Jason Aronson Publishers, by the generous permission of the author
- Dr. Peter Pitzele, *Scripture Windows: Bibliodrama*, by the generous permission of the author
- Aliza Arzt, "Role Playing at the Seder," by the generous permission of the author
- Israel Eldad, *Chronicles*, by permission of his widow, Batya Washitz, and the Arrow Company
- Joe Buchwald Gelles, "Myths About Egypt and the Hebrews," by permission of the author

Chapter 8 —
- Hayyim Schauss, "Marranos Observe Passover," *Passover Anthology*, edited by Philip Goodman
- Paul Cowan, *An Orphan in History*
- Micha Odenheimer, oral history of Ethiopia, 1991 in an interview with the editor
- Danny Siegel, *My Parents' Personal Passover Ritual*, by generous permission of the author
- Rabbi Mark Greenspan, *Sharing Family Memories*, by generous permission of the author

Chapter 9 — Danny Siegel, *"The Four Children,"* by generous permission of the author

Chapter 10 — Ben Shahn, *No Man Can Command My Conscience*, by permission of Ben Shahn Estate/Licensed by VAGA, NY, NY

Chapter 11 —
- Stuart Schoffman, "Tales of Red Matza," Jerusalem Report, April 4, 1991
- Franz Rosenzweig, *The Star of Redemption*, translated by William Hallo ©1964, 1970, 1971, by permission of Henry Holt and Co.

Chapter 12 —
- Professor David Hartman, essays from transcripts of Hebrew University lectures on holidays by permission of the lecturer
- Professor David Hartman, *"Memory and Values, Joy and Responsibility"* (Posner, 1978), by permission of the author

Chapter 13 — Professor Nahum Sarna, *Exploring Exodus*, ©1986, by permission of Shocken Books/Random House/Pantheon

Chapter 14 — Dr. Michael Walzer, *Exodus and Revolution*, ©1985 by Basic Books, Inc. Reprinted by permission of Basic Books, a division of Harper Collins Publishers, Inc.

Chapter 15 — Professor Julius Lester, *"Here am I,"* New Traditions, by permission of the author

Chapter 16 — Rabbi David Golinkin, *"Moses and Herzl,"* Conservative Judaism Vol. 47 #1 (Fall, 1994) by permission of the author without footnotes and with abbreviated summation

Notes and References for
Preparing for Seder Night: A Practical Manual (pp. 7-15)

1. T. B. Pesachim 115b
2. T. B. Pesachim 114b
3. Menachem Kasher, Haggadah Shleima, p. 65; Masei Rokeah #59
4. Shivlei HaLeket reports a strange addition to charoset: a little clay or the scrapings off a brick. Other rabbis rejected this custom out of hand — M. Kasher, p.64
5. HaRokeah 284 in M. Kasher, p. 63; Maimonides' Commentary on the Mishnah in M. Kasher, p. 63
6. Back on Tur O.H. 473
7. Daniel Goldschmidt, *The Haggadah*, pp. 76-77
8. T. B. Avodah Zara 11
9. T. B. Pesachim 98b
10. Shivlei HaLeket, Menachem Kasher, p. 67
11. Rabbi Moshe Sternbach, Haggadah of the Vilna Gaon
12. Daniel Sperber, Minhagei Yisrael, Vol. IV, p. 170
13. Avi HaEzri, Kasher (above)
14. Aruch Hashulchan O.H. 470, Rabbi Ovadya Josef, Chazon Ovadia, pp. 96-97

Acknowledgements to the Designer

Joe Buchwald Gelles was the imaginative designer of *The Leader's Guide* as well as the relentless production manager of both the *Haggadah* and the *Leader's Guide*. His contribution was absolutely essential in the whole project.